IMAGES
of America

RINCON POINT

This aerial photograph from about 1929 shows the wave refraction that would make Rincon Point a globally renowned surfing spot. Note the hairpin curve of the highway to the right of the more gentle curve of the railroad tracks, the site of many auto accidents. Japanese-born farmer Kijuro Ota raised cantaloupe and other crops in the fields to the right of the highway. Around the time that this picture was taken, Robert W. Bates and his brother Edward purchased much of the beachfront at lower right from the Hill family. The sale included a roadhouse-hotel just below the highway turn. A year or two later, Robert Bates built a ranch house on the bald mesa (above the train tracks and highway, seen here with two structures), using bricks from a brickyard on Rincon Creek, and moved his family from their beach cottage. (Courtesy Burpee family.)

ON THE COVER: In 1951, surf legend Dick Metz captured friends (from left to right) Gene McCafferty, Joe Riddick, Dick Barr, and an unidentified cigarette-smoker at Rincon Point. These exuberant surfers were among the first to rediscover the point after World War II. The massive wooden board pictured here is "scarfed" (the front end has been lifted to improve maneuverability), an innovation by design legend Bob Simmons. Metz found his way to Santa Barbara in the early 1950s to attend what was then the Santa Barbara College of the University of California. Like many following in his bare footsteps, he picked Santa Barbara for his studies mostly because of the excellent surf. This and the other Metz photographs here are some of the earliest available depictions of surf culture at Rincon. (Courtesy Dick Metz/Surfing Heritage and Culture Center Archives.)

IMAGES
of America

RINCON POINT

Vincent Burns and Stephen Bates

ARCADIA
PUBLISHING

Published by Arcadia Publishing
Charleston, South Carolina

Printed in the United States of America

Library of Congress Control Number: 2022942874

For all general information, please contact Arcadia Publishing:
Telephone 843-853-2070
Fax 843-853-0044
E-mail sales@arcadiapublishing.com
For customer service and orders:
Toll-Free 1-888-313-2665

Visit us on the Internet at www.arcadiapublishing.com

To Charlotte, Al, Hadley, and Clara.
—S.B.

To all Rincon lovers, past, present, and future.
—V.B.

CONTENTS

ACKNOWLEDGMENTS

While we are grateful to everyone who shared photographs, documents, and anecdotes, we are especially indebted to Charlotte Meryman, Marsha Ota, Steve Halsted, Andy Neumann, Doug White, Debby Burns, and Jim Campos, who gave us access to troves of material, referred us to other sources, and helped fact-check the manuscript.

We also received important information and images from Suzanne Bates Ward, Robbie Hutto, Ed McKay, John W. Evans and family, the Burpee family, the Lewis family, the Ramirez family, Johnny Brown, Tony Brown, Don Balch, and Steve Bissell, as well as David Griggs of the Carpinteria Valley Museum of History, Chris Ervin of the Gledhill Library at the Santa Barbara Historical Museum, founder Dick Metz of the Surfing Heritage and Culture Center in San Clemente, Mauricio Gomez, John Johnson of the Santa Barbara Natural History Museum, Matt Warshaw of the online Encyclopedia of Surfing, Deya Terrafranca of the Museum of Ventura County, Marla Daily of the Santa Cruz Island Foundation, Helen P. Rydell of the Santa Barbara County Genealogical Society, and Susie Skarl and Yuko Shinozaki of Lied Library at the University of Nevada, Las Vegas.

For reading and commenting on portions of the manuscript, we thank Polly Bates, Doug White, and Andy Neumann.

INTRODUCTION

Before the Beach Boys released "Surfin' U.S.A.," in which the band name-checked Rincon to a national audience, it was already a famous surf spot. Before the print and film versions of *Gidget* created modern surf culture, rebellious youth were gathering at the point to build fires, surf the waves, and camp on the beach.

But surfing arrived late in the history of Rincon Point. Indeed, the name Rincon Point arrived relatively late. The Chumash called it Shuku. Spanish soldiers in 1769 named it Pueblo del Bailarín, "Village of the Dancer," in honor of an Indian there. Spanish soldiers in 1772 conferred a new name, El Rincón, "The Corner." By around 1900, some called the area Benham, after a Southern Pacific Railroad stop nearby. Others called the promontory Hill's Point, in honor of a family living near the mouth of the creek. Hill's Point and Benham faded. Rincon Point endured.

There were many names, and so, too, there were many nationalities. The first person to hold legal title to Rincon Point, in 1835, was a former soldier born in Spanish California, Teodoro Arellanes. Just as the Spanish had taken the point from the Chumash, the American government tried to take it from Arellanes, unsuccessfully. Those who played roles in its subsequent development include physicians from England and Peru, a druggist from Chile, a Japanese farmer, a French war bride, and a Swedish actor famous for playing a Chinese detective.

If a time-lapse video condensed the history of Rincon Point into a few minutes, it would look something like this:

The Chumash and their predecessors live and fish there for millennia, with the village moving closer to the ocean as their plank *tomols* grow more important for fishing and trading. Their population in 1769 is approximately 300, which drops to zero when the Spanish move them to missions. Starting in the 1830s, the Arellanes family grazes cattle and horses in the area. Stagecoaches pass by starting in the 1860s, trains in the 1880s, and autos in the 1900s, all with difficulty at first; steep bluffs on one side and the sea on the other make for treacherous travel just east of the point, on the way to Ventura. (One of the unusual features of the region is that the coastline runs mainly east-west rather than north-south.) In laying tracks, the Southern Pacific Railroad constructs a retaining wall and redirects Rincon Creek.

Starting in the 1870s, archeologists dig up Chumash relics. In 1875, neighbors dig up the body of John C. Norton, victim of a love-triangle murder. For decades starting in the 1880s, treasure-hunters dig futilely for Joaquin Murietta's chest of diamonds, which is said to be buried by an oak tree marked with a cross. Starting in the 1890s, the Hill family raises crops on Rincon Point, but in 1914, the rain-swollen creek knocks down the Southern Pacific retaining wall and wipes out their farmhouse. The railroad buys them a new house on higher ground.

In 1919, Robert W. Bates arrives at Rincon Point after a stint in the ambulance service in Europe during World War I. (A subordinate, Lt. Ernest Hemingway, disliked him.) Accompanied by his new wife, a nurse who cared for him in a Paris hospital when he had appendicitis, Bates finds a scraggly assortment of sand dunes, a squatter's shack, a wooden automobile causeway, and, incongruously, a louche hotel on Hill family property. Bates ejects the squatter, builds himself a $400 cottage, tries but fails to make a living raising lima beans and hay, and recruits Japanese-born Kijuro Ota to take over the farming. The Bateses keep livestock on Rincon Point, as do the Hills and the Otas.

Prohibition begins, the hotel gets raided, and its manager goes to jail. The state replaces the causeway with a road behind a seawall. A brickyard opens just up Rincon Creek, which produces pastel-colored bricks. New cottages get built, and, in the wake of floods, old cottages get dragged to new locations, including the Bates one. Under a series of managers, the hotel keeps getting raided. Oil derricks rise and fall. On the hillside, the so-called volcano spews smoke.

In the 1920s, Robert Bates and his brother Edward buy beachfront west of Rincon Creek from the Hills. Edward builds himself a house there and a bridge to reach it. In the 1940s, the Army brings in a motley garrison and a shore gun. The state widens the highway and eliminates the hotel. In the 1950s, the Bates family markets beach houses at "exclusive Rincon Del Mar," priced from $15,500 to $45,000. Buyers—many from Pasadena—build vacation homes. They share interests, including a love of the ocean and, in some cases, a rotating 5:00 p.m. cocktail hour. In the 1960s, the state widens the highway again, in the process layering concrete and asphalt over Chumash graves. Offshore oil derricks and even an "oil island" appear, one disgorges a massive spill in 1969, and then, they very slowly recede.

In the 1970s, a Ventura developer buys the last empty tract on Rincon Point and builds 14 houses. In the same decade, a Santa Barbara developer buys what is known as the Hill estate. The ramshackle homes and shacks populated by bohemians and eccentrics on the point's west side are replaced with orderly condominiums. On both halves of the point, many of the modest cottages from the 1920s and 1930s are razed and replaced by more imposing structures.

A "greatest generation" of Rincon surfers assembles at Rincon Point in 1966 for an iconic photograph and then disperses, some to Hawaii, one to Vietnam. Rincon's waves become a testing ground for innovators like George Greenough and Renny Yater. The boards become shorter, and the riders are now occasionally women. The association between Rincon and surfing eventually produces a tidal wave of branding, including a local brewery and surf shop. And why not? Attaching yourself to the elegance of Rincon's waves is straight out of Business 101.

Near the beginning of the 20th century, the Bates family owned 755 acres of Rancho El Rincon, which they called Rincon del Mar. According to Edward Bates, the 30 or so acres of Rincon Point seemed virtually worthless—subject to erosion and littered with debris from ocean and creek. At century's end, Rincon Point is far more valuable than the other 700-odd acres of what was Rincon del Mar. The patch of sand dunes has turned into a posh gated community worth hundreds of millions of dollars.

Although a few families manage to keep their Rincon homes over two or more generations, others get displaced. In the latest act in this process, second- and third-generation Rinconers, whose professional-class forebears purchased homes and lots beginning in the 1940s, risk being supplanted by a yet-wealthier class of buyers, as property and estate taxes take their toll.

Yet the past is never entirely obliterated. A resident in 1988 digs a koi pond and finds a Chumash skeleton. In the early 2000s, another resident sees errant asparagus shoots, which he thinks are sprouting from century-old seeds from the Hill farm. Decades after the brickyard closed, pastel-colored bricks continue washing up on the beach after storms.

The United States has 265 Rincon place names, including Rincon Points in San Francisco and South Texas, but the Rincon Point that straddles Santa Barbara and Ventura Counties is unique, a small promontory with a long and rich history.

One

PREHISTORIC SHUKU

According to Edward Bates, "Between the ocean and highway, the soil of Rincon Point is a strange, black mixture of sand, pulverized seafood shells, and charcoal fire ash, proof the Chumash Indian tribe lived on the ground for many years before the calamitous invasion of the white man. The point is an ideal aboriginal campsite with fresh water in the creek, and surf never too high to launch fishing canoes. Arrowheads, beads, pestles, and mortars are numerous, but few people bother to look for them."

Bates accurately described the ideal nature of the site and the quantity of artifacts created by the point's prehistoric residents. And excavations have probed Rincon's "strange mixture" for almost 150 years. One of the first excavators, Stephen Bowers in 1884, was struck by the size of the settlement at Rincon and stated, "At least a hundred acres are covered with shells, bones, fish scales, and other kitchen debris of the Indians who have lived here from time immemorial." Besides thousands of artifacts, excavations have also turned up skeletal remains in the hundreds. Equally impressive, investigations into prehistoric Rincon's many layers suggest that the Rincon site has witnessed approximately 10,000 years of continuous human settlement, a stunning length of time.

The name prehistoric (and historic) residents gave to Rincon was Shuku. Mission baptismal documents contain the names of numerous Shuku residents and show connections between the village and other known prehistoric sites, including on the Channel Islands. Unfortunately, modern alterations to the point's original topography and changes in modern attitudes about archaeological excavations and artifacts make it likely the era of major excavations and discoveries at Rincon Point is over.

Artifacts like these turned up frequently at the point in the past, especially in the "meadow" area developed in the late 1970s. In fact, large artifacts like these were so common in the early 20th century that they presented a nuisance to anyone plowing the meadow. Archaeologists usually date artifacts like the mortars and pestles here to a more recent period of Shuku since they often occur in the upper four feet of excavation pits. (Courtesy private party.)

Here is a portion of a steatite (soapstone) bowl found at Rincon during an archaeological excavation. Steatite is a talc-schist metamorphic rock that can be easily carved. Archaeologists believe this and other steatite artifacts were originally produced at Santa Catalina Island, which has an outcrop of the stone, and made their way to Rincon via trade. Bowls like this were prized because they could be placed directly over fire. (Courtesy Santa Barbara Natural History Museum.)

Here is a steatite smoking pipe found at Rincon Point. Although this one is of exceptional quality, smoking pipes are common at Chumash sites. Archaeologists believe the pipes—which likely held a wild tobacco—were used on ceremonial occasions. Like the other steatite artifacts at Rincon, this pipe likely documents a trade network with the wider Chumash world, including the Channel Islands. (Courtesy Santa Barbara Natural History Museum.)

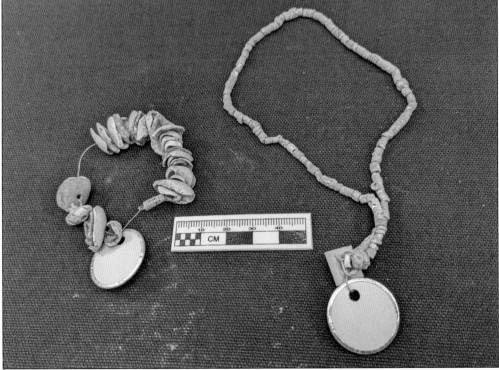

Here are two shell strings from Rincon. The necklace at right contains beads that have been laboriously manufactured from olivella shells using chert drilling tools. Scholars now believe that olivella beads, manufactured on Santa Cruz Island, served as a form of currency throughout the prehistoric Chumash world, a startling discovery since hunter-gatherers were presumed to have no need for money. (Courtesy Santa Barbara Natural History Museum.)

Four chert projectile points from Rincon Point are pictured. Most chert found on the mainland is associated with the Franciscan Complex, a formation of rocks found in California's Coast Range. Prehistoric peoples worked chert rocks to create razor sharp points for knives, arrows, spears, and many other tools. (Courtesy Santa Barbara Natural History Museum.)

In 1988, digging for a koi pond at Rincon unearthed an ancient skeleton. A brouhaha ensued as Ventura County authorities first told the homeowner to pay the costs of having the skeleton and artifacts analyzed and then gave him the opportunity to simply return the site to its original condition. In the end, the site was excavated as shown here, revealing midden deposits with olivella beads, some drilled with metal needles, indicating the site was occupied during the historical Mission Period. The skeleton was of a male at least 40 years old. (Courtesy Santa Barbara Natural History Museum.)

Two

CALIFORNIOS AND IMMIGRANTS

None of the earliest owners of Rancho El Rincon, which included Rincon Point, was born under the American flag. In 1835, the Mexican government of Alta California deeded the rancho to Teodoro Arellanes, who had been baptized at Mission Santa Clara in 1782, during Spanish rule. In 1855, Arellanes conveyed the property to Mateo Henry Biggs, born to English parents in Peru. In 1885, Biggs sold it to a Chilean, Benigno Gutierrez, in partnership with an Englishman, Charles Bell Bates. Although all four visited the ranch, none of them lived there. Arellanes was a rancher with extensive holdings. Biggs and Bates were physicians, and Gutierrez was a druggist in the small town (population roughly 4,000 in 1870) of Santa Barbara.

It was a town in transition, with Californios—those born there during Spanish or Mexican rule—losing their ascendancy. Nearly all surnames in Santa Barbara were Spanish in 1852; fewer than a third were in 1870. Under Spain and Mexico, the town had evolved in the style of a European village, with scattered adobes connected by meandering paths. After the Americans took control in 1848, they imposed a grid, with straight streets intersecting at right angles. If a house extended into the new thoroughfare, the roadbuilders demolished it. Californios, said Pablo de la Guerra of Santa Barbara, had become "strangers on the very soil on which we were native."

Under the treaty that ended the Mexican-American War in 1848, the United States pledged to respect property titles established under Mexican law. With the Gold Rush, however, California's population jumped from 14,000 in 1848 to 93,000 in 1850 and 380,000 in 1860, and the newcomers wanted land. Against this backdrop, the United States implemented an arduous process for validating property titles established under Mexican law. Whenever an owner fell short or gave up, land became available for settlers.

Between 1835, when Arellanes received Rancho El Rincon, and 1885, when Biggs sold it to Gutierrez and Bates, Santa Barbara and Carpinteria changed a great deal, but Rincon Point remained largely the same—oaks, sycamores, and sand dunes, bisected by a creek, with cliffs on either side. What it did not have was people.

The first person to hold title to Rincon Point was Teodoro Arellanes (spelled various ways). Born in Mission Santa Clara in 1782, according to mission records, Arellanes grew up in the Presidio of Santa Barbara and served as a soldier. After leaving the military, he became one of the wealthiest ranchers in the area—by one estimate, only William Welles Hollister was richer—with some 20,000 head of cattle. Arellanes owned Rancho El Rincon, which was just over 4,428 acres (one square Spanish league), and he co-owned, with Diego Olivera, Rancho de Guadalupe near Santa Maria, which was much bigger at 43,682 acres. According to contemporaries, Arellanes was courtly and refined. Like many others, he was also illiterate. Documents concerning the Rancho El Rincon land grant bear his X. (Courtesy Curletti [Rosario] Collection, Gledhill Library, Santa Barbara Historical Museum.)

Teodoro Arellanes married Maria Josefa Andrea Rodriguez in 1805. They had 11 children, born between 1808 and 1835. All six of his daughters had Maria as a first or middle name, including these three, from left to right, Maria de los Reyes, Maria Ignacia, and Maria Jesus Rita. (Maria Jesus Rita's marriage to Mateo H. Biggs in 1853 would open a new chapter in the history of Rancho El Rincon.) As a little girl, one Arellanes daughter supposedly would show playmates a trunk full of gold coins. "You can have one," she would say. "Papa has lots of them." Maria del Carmen Gutierrez Hill, born in Santa Barbara in 1859, a daughter of Benigno Gutierrez, heard that story and passed it along to Robert W. Bates in the 1930s. (Courtesy Dolores Pelton and Rancho de Guadalupe Historical Society.)

In 1833 and again in 1835, Teodoro Arellanes asked the governor of Alta California for "the place named 'Rincon,' " where he proposed to put 500 cattle, 120 horses, and "more than nine children" (he had additional ones on the way). Arellanes described the property as running "from the Arroyo de los Sauces to the Arroyo de la Brea in length, and from the Arroyo de las Casitas to the beach as its breadth, that is two leagues in length and one in breadth." This is understood to mean from Los Sauces Creek (between Faria Beach and Mussel Shoals) west to Carpinteria Creek, and from Casitas Creek south to the Pacific. Arellanes submitted this map to the governor's office. No. 7, at bottom right, is described as "the edge of the thicket" that reaches the beach, perhaps Rincon Point. The governor deeded Rancho El Rincon to Arellanes in 1835, one of the earliest land grants in what is now Santa Barbara County. (Courtesy Bancroft Library, University of California, Berkeley.)

Through attorney Henry Wager Halleck, shown here, Teodoro Arellanes petitioned the US government to confirm his ownership of Rancho El Rincon in 1852. Under the Treaty of Guadalupe Hidalgo of 1848, the United States pledged that property rights established during Mexican rule "shall be inviolably respected." The process for validating ownership, however, was burdensome and arbitrary. (Courtesy Library of Congress.)

Government attorney Pacificus Ord tried to invalidate Teodoro Arellanes's claim to Rancho El Rincon. Ord threw in every argument he could devise: the map was unclear, the interim governor who signed the land grant was a usurper, and the deed bore the wrong stamps. Ultimately, Arellanes lost before the federal Land Commission but won in court. (Courtesy Booth Family Center for Special Collections, Georgetown University Library.)

Born in Peru to English parents, Mateo Henry Biggs came to California in 1848 and settled in Santa Barbara in 1851. He farmed, raised cattle, traded land, and practiced medicine, belatedly earning a medical degree in 1870. In his spare time, he liked to hypnotize his servants and try to make crosses and stigmata appear on their skin. In 1853, Biggs married Maria Jesus Rita Arellanes. The union may have been unhappy—he told a bachelor friend that "you are a very lucky man to have escaped matrimony"—but it proved lucrative; his wife's father, Teodoro Arellanes, deeded Rancho El Rincon to him in 1855. After the federal government dropped its appeal in 1857, Biggs owned an unsurveyed tract of no more than 4,428 acres (one square Spanish league) under the district court's ruling, though a federal survey in 1860 certified 4,460 acres. Biggs went on to sell hundreds of acres to early Carpinteria settlers such as the Bailards, Pysters, and Walkers. On visits to the Rincon ranch, according to local historian Georgia Stockton, Biggs delighted in eating prickly pear. (Courtesy Bates family.)

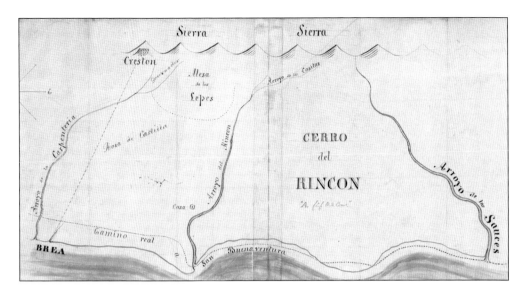

As defined in the land grant of 1835, Rancho El Rincon formed a rough half circle, as shown on the c. 1855 map above. The United States certified the tract shown on the 1860 survey below. The original grant was bigger, extending south to the ocean along Los Sauces Creek, which, according to the surveyor's notes from 1860, lay about a mile and a quarter beyond the dividing ridge used as the eastern boundary, but, contrary to lore, it did not extend from Montecito to Ventura. Mateo Biggs, who completed the certification process, claimed that he could have gotten a much bigger tract if he had offered a bribe of $550. It is not clear whom he might have bribed. It may have been Pacificus Ord, who is known to have enriched himself while serving as a federal attorney. (Above, courtesy Bancroft Library, University of California, Berkeley; below, courtesy Ventura County Surveyor.)

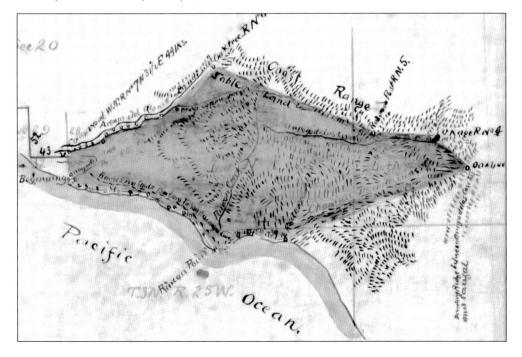

Benigno Gutierrez emigrated from Chile to California during the Gold Rush in 1849. After mining, farming, and trading cattle in various towns, he bumped into a friend from Latin America, Mateo H. Biggs. Biggs settled in Santa Barbara in 1851, and Gutierrez followed in about 1854. For $125, they bought the deck cabin from an old shipwreck, moved it downtown, and opened the Gutierrez Drugstore. (Business may have been slow. According to Santa Barbara County supervisors' minutes for 1856, Benigno Gutierrez collected $17.75 from the indigent and sick fund.) Later, Biggs erected Apothecaries Hall, Santa Barbara's first brick building, and the drugstore moved there. Biggs returned to Latin America in 1873. In 1885, he sold his remaining holdings in Rancho El Rincon to Gutierrez and Charles Bell Bates for $10,000. Biggs had already sold much of the ranch piecemeal, and it appears that Gutierrez and Bates got roughly half of the original 4,460-acre tract. (Courtesy Bates family.)

In 1890, Dr. Reuben Webb Hill, a Civil War veteran, bought part of Rancho El Rincon in Santa Barbara County, including the western portion of Rincon Point. Near the mouth of Rincon Creek, he built a house and planted asparagus, bell peppers, and chili. He appears to have been the first owner to live full-time on Rincon Point, and for a few years, it was known as Hill's Point. He was also the first owner born under the American flag, in Vermont. (Courtesy Suzanne Rhodes.)

Dr. Hill died in 1912. This undated photograph shows his widow, Maria del Carmen Gutierrez Hill, who was a daughter of Benigno Gutierrez. She died in 1937. (Courtesy Suzanne Rhodes.)

Carpinteria experienced cataclysmic floods in 1914, with an estimated eight inches of rain falling in 36 hours. On Rincon Creek, a Southern Pacific Railroad retaining wall collapsed, and the Hill family house, barn, and outbuildings all were swept out to sea. The railroad later paid the Hills $7,000. Here, members of the family pose at the site of the devastation. Maria Del Carmen Hill, daughter of Benigno Gutierrez, is in the back. At right is her daughter Carmelita. The family rebuilt on higher ground. One of Dr. Hill's sons, Edwin, grew corn and tomatoes and kept pigs and chickens on Rincon Point. Another son, James, ran a filling station on the highway. Daughters Carmelita Hill Rhodes and Esolina Hill West also lived on the point. (Courtesy Suzanne Rhodes.)

Three

THE LAND EVOLVES

The arrival of reliable coastal passage between Ventura and Santa Barbara ended Rincon Point's isolation, eventually paving the way for luxury beach homes, surfers, a homeowner association, and everything else to follow. The Hill and Bates families were the first to build significant housing on Rincon Point. And they were also the first to see the same houses destroyed or damaged by flood. The former built a stately home on the point in the 19th century that a 1914 flood destroyed, while Robert W. Bates built cottages too close to the creek that were nearly carried off to sea in 1926. The Hills rebuilt, and their home dominated the point's west side until its demolition. Robert's brother Edward built his house on high ground in 1929. Once the creek was dependably bridged, a mini-boom occurred on the west side as families like the Verondas and Thachers bought property. Just before and then after World War II, there was another small boom, mostly on the point's Ventura side. The early 1970s saw the purchase for development of the last beachfront lots. Two final projects, overseen by professional developers, filled in the last off-water empty spots: the "meadow" and the Colony. After that, new houses could only come about through the demolition and replacement of their predecessors, an ongoing process. This chapter provides a visual record of all these changes to the land. The images move from a wide-angle view of the point to close-ups of individual lots and houses. Photographs illustrate the gradual evolution of Rincon from a near-pristine and isolated 30-acre "corner" of California to the densely packed residential and recreational "Queen of the Coast" in place since the 1970s and now collectively worth several hundreds of millions of dollars.

The east side of Rincon Point was photographed by John Peabody Harrington (1884–1961) around midsummer 1923. A towering figure in the history of American anthropology, Harrington dedicated his life to the languages, cultures, and customs of Native Americans, particularly in California. His research came at a time when Chumash culture was disappearing, along with its native speakers, who Harrington painstakingly recorded. This and the following photograph were found among Harrington's papers at the Smithsonian and were taken in conjunction with his Chumash investigations in the 1920s. His excavation at Burton Mound, a large Chumash site in Santa Barbara, represented his main current interest, although he also had time for research excursions, in this case to Rincon Point. Harrington's photograph looks east, showing Punta Gorda and Pitas Point. At left, just south of the railroad tracks, is a small hill with a collection of utility poles. Toward the center, on the east side of Rincon Creek, are three white buildings likely built by the Bates family, including two that were to suffer in the 1926 flood. To the west (right) is the "meadow," just beginning to be worked by the Otas. At the far right are buildings associated with the Hill family. (Smithsonian Institution.)

This western portion of John Peabody Harrington's 1923 Rincon Point panorama photograph highlights the agricultural nature of Rincon Point at the time. Despite his frantic drive, Harrington's peripatetic ways made it difficult for him to bring projects to publication. Instead, he left behind great masses of notes, unpublished reports, artifacts, hundreds of feet of files, and several tons of boxes of other material, most of which is now at the Smithsonian Institution. Despite the quantity and confusing nature of the materials, the Harrington collection is a gold mine for anthropologists and many others interested in Native America. In the summer of 1923, besides conducting the Burton Mound excavation, Harrington also oversaw the construction by Chumash Indians of a grass lodge for exhibition at the Ventura County Fair. In between these tasks, the ethnologist worked on a plan with field director David Banks Rogers to explore systematically the archaeology along the Santa Barbara coast. In this photograph, an oil derrick is prominent, as are farm buildings likely associated with the Hill family portion of Rincon Point. The white shapes below and to the right of the derrick are drying laundry. On either side of the creek can be seen sand dunes or Chumash middens. The beach itself is little changed from today's view, with a low tide exposing the rocks and tide pools at the point. (Smithsonian Institution.)

The dramatic c. 1930 photograph above, taken looking southeast, shows the area before development. It includes the outcrops running from Carpinteria to Ventura as well as citrus trees and the rugged backcountry inland along Rincon Creek. Visible in succession from the center to the top are Rincon Point, Punta Gorda (also known as Mussel Shoals and "Little Rincon"), Pitas Point, and the Ventura River mouth. Below is a very early photograph, taken around 1916, of the beach at Rincon Point. The mouth of Rincon Creek is just visible, and on the other (west) side are Chumash middens or sand dunes. (Above, courtesy Edson Smith Photo Collection; below, courtesy Stephenson family.)

Here is new construction at the point in the 1930s. Pictured above behind the hotel are the early bridge, home, and "carriage house" of Edward Bates on the west side of Rincon Creek. This new construction replaced the oil derricks, which were destroyed in a bonfire remembered by Bobby Bates. The Bates beach house and cabin occupied by uncle Harry Mitchell visible in earlier photographs are now missing, likely relocated to the east. Pictured below is Edward Bates's house at 181 Rincon Point Road. According to Robert W. Bates, writing in March 1929, Edward "is still at work on his beach cottage which is nearing completion. It is a very attractive little house & he has got a great kick out of building it." The home still stands, having had several owners since Edward and Julia Bates departed for Santa Barbara. (Above, courtesy Burns family; below, courtesy Biddle/Boyle family.)

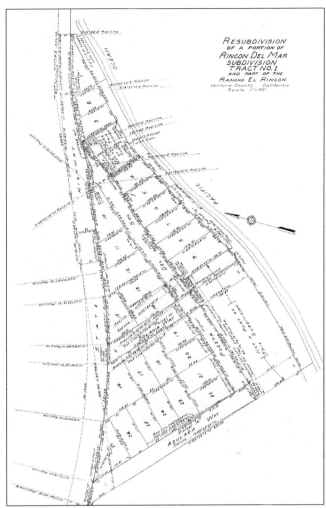

Plans created in July 1926 by Robert W. Bates and submitted to Ventura County contemplated a substantial 32-lot development on the point's east side. It is not known why the project did not move forward, but the arrival of the Great Depression probably played a role. In the end, the eastern interior (the "meadow," land farmed by the Otas) was finally developed in the 1970s. It consisted of about 14 homes, a smaller version of Bates's early vision. One can only imagine how different the point would look today if this project had gone forward instead of Rincon being developed piecemeal. (Both, courtesy Doug White.)

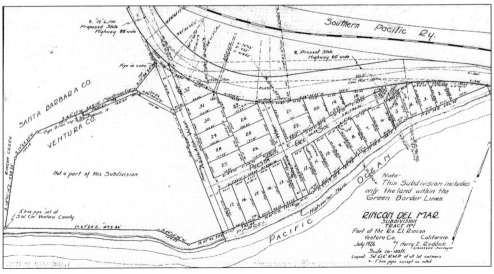

This 1935 photograph looks north toward the Bates Ranch from the dunes on the west side of the creek. The south face of the hotel and accompanying water tank and palm trees are visible, as is a portion of Edward Bates's early bridge and various buildings, probably belonging to the Ota family. Between the cottages and the outhouse in the foreground are laundry and a person. (Courtesy Bates family.)

This 1943 photograph highlights homes on the point's east side. From bottom to top are an early house at the end of Puesta del Sol where it once met the highway, and the Dolman (8072 Puesta del Sol) and Diedrich (8078 Puesta del Sol) houses, both built around 1935. The Bates Cottage (8134 Puesta del Sol) is probably the white house just visible on higher ground east of the creek. At top right is the hotel. (Courtesy Lewis family.)

Above, road building takes place around 1937. Bobby Bates said, "I graded the roadbed—behind the lots—with a 'Fresno scraper.' " Edward Bates remembered, "This shows the cutting of Rincon Point Road, July 1937. Waldo Ramirez is driving the team, with a Filipino helper." About the beachcomber shack visible in both photographs, one Rincon resident wrote, "I never did know who lived in that little shack . . . the man drew enough oil from the ground with a little pump to use it for lighting. And he must have used it for cooking too. The house was nestled up next to the knoll which must have been the lot to the east of the [David and Juliette] Greys' house." Edward Bates recalled demolishing the shack around 1937. (Above, courtesy Stephenson family; below, courtesy Bates family.)

Here is the Thacher house, built in 1940. This photograph was taken in January 1949 after a long-remembered storm dumped snow throughout Southern California. Elisa Blake Thacher (1872–1944), wife of Thacher School founder Sherman Day Thacher, purchased the lot from the Bates family around 1938 for $3,000 and had noted architect Austen Pierpont design and build the beach house. Of simple board-and-batten construction, the home stands strong and is owned and jointly enjoyed by many members of the Thacher clan. (Courtesy Thacher family.)

This aerial photograph was taken after 1951 and shows the Edward Bates house in the center, Rincon Point Road below it, the white creek-side Peck House at 196 Rincon Point Road (built in 1951), and across the creek, the home at 8134 Puesta del Sol (built in 1940). At lower left is 140 Rincon Point Road (built in 1949), then the farthest east of the oceanfront homes on the Santa Barbara side of the creek. (Courtesy Biddle/Boyle family.)

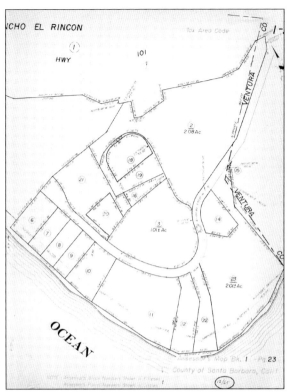

On this 1965 county assessor map for Rincon's Santa Barbara County side, each numbered lot corresponds to a property tax assessment. To the northwest is Hill family land. Of the lots on the beach, Nos. 6 to 12 were owned respectively by the McCaskeys, Modisettes, the Anson Thachers, Elizabeth Thacher, Claire Veronda, the Bates family, and David and Juliette Grey. No. 22 was also owned by the Greys. No. 23 was owned by the Bates family. (Courtesy André Luthard.)

This 1970 Caltrans photograph shows highway construction. The massive project was a seminal event in the history of Rincon Point, including widening and rerouting the freeway, adding a county park and state beach on either side of the point, and removing five million cubic yards of soil from the hillside. At bottom left is Hill family land on the point's west side. (Courtesy California Department of Transportation.)

These two photographs are likely from the 1970s. At right is the stately home built by Juliette and David Grey in the late 1950s. This was the first two-story home on the point's oceanfront west side. Earlier deeds required that homes not exceed a single story. For a few years, the Greys' house dominated the point's west side, until the following properties to its east went for sale: 182 Rincon Point Road (built in 1976), 180 Rincon Point Road (built in 1977), and 176 Rincon Point (built in 1989). In the c. 1977 aerial photograph below, a second seawall has been added to the east of the Greys' house, and homes in the "meadow" are in the midst of construction on the east side. The lots to the east of 140 Rincon Point Road have yet to be developed. (Right, courtesy Burns family; below, courtesy Bates family.)

Pictured above, Santa Barbara architect Peter Edwards (1924–2018) and Helen Norton Andreson (1907–1996) examine sketches for 180 Rincon Point Road (finished 1977), one of the last oceanfront lots at Rincon Point. They are crouching near the former sand dunes to the west of the creek mouth. The lot, purchased from the Bates family in 1973, cost $80,000. The bill of sale included the requirement that the sellers cap an oil well on the property, likely associated with derricks seen in photographs from the 1920s. Pictured below is the development of the "meadow" on the east side of the point, behind the beachfront homes on Puesta del Sol. This was the likely site of prehistoric Shuku and where the Otas farmed. By 1980, about 14 homes were added to Rincon Point on Puesta del Sol and Buena Fortuna Roads. (Above, courtesy Burns family; below, courtesy Bates family.)

The most significant causes of topographical change at Rincon was the construction of 70-odd homes during the 20th century and the massive widening and alteration of Highway 101 and the associated creation of public areas between it and the point's private property. Despite pre-construction archaeological digs in the late 1960s, these giant projects likely destroyed or disturbed many undiscovered artifacts. Above, job site superintendent Barney Connaughton surveys progress, while below the enormity of the undertaking is visible in this photograph taken just west and north of the point. (Above, courtesy Judy Connaughton; below, courtesy Carpinteria Valley Museum of History.)

This aerial photograph from August 1, 1929, features tree-lined Rincon Creek running slightly diagonally from the top to the coast, reaching the sand to the right (eastern) side of the point after passing underneath the railroad and highway. The point itself remains largely in its natural state. On the west side, the Hill homes and a beachcomber shack may just be discerned. On the east side are two clusters of houses. Also on the east side are the tidy fields maintained by the Otas at this time. (Courtesy UCSB Library Geospatial Collection.)

The scene here is a long way from the desolate oceanfront and squatter shacks that greeted Robert Bates and his new wife in 1919. This 2001 aerial photograph shows Rincon Point largely in its current state with 70-odd homes, the 101 freeway and ramps, and current county park and state beach. The final two acts in the development of the modern point are now complete—the building out of the "meadow" (between Puesta del Sol and the highway) and the Colony on former Hill family land. By 2002, the two founding families of modern Rincon Point, the Bateses and the Hills, no longer owned any land or homes on Rincon Point. Although a handful of homes could lay claim to pre–World War II construction, many were built since the 1960s. Most of the point's early structures have been demolished and gone the way of ancient Shuku, with traces only visible in old photographs and historical documents. (Courtesy UCSB Library Geospatial Collection.)

Four

A FOUNDING FAMILY

Several dozen members of the Bates family shared in the ownership of Rincon Point, but three men were principally responsible for shaping the place: Dr. Charles Bell Bates, who bought the property in 1885, and his sons Robert and Edward, who developed it from the 1920s to the 1970s.

Charles Bell Bates was an 18-year-old student at King's College London in 1860 when his father summoned him to the goldfields of California. He probably anticipated a brief Wild West sojourn and then a return to England. Instead, he ended up spending the rest of his life in the United States, mainly Santa Barbara, where he practiced medicine, married a fellow Briton, and bought and sold real estate. In 1885, Dr. Bates and a partner paid $10,000 for roughly 2,000 acres of Rancho El Rincon, including Rincon Point. The seller was Mateo Henry Biggs, Dr. Bates's former medical partner. Biggs had already sold the best parcels of the ranch piecemeal. Now, he was glad to unload what remained of, in his words, "that confounded Rincon ranch."

For Dr. Bates's son Robert Wentworth Bates, too, California was not part of the original plan. He grew up in Santa Barbara, attended a boarding school in England followed by Groton and Harvard, and went to work for a Boston piano company that his family co-owned. He later wrote that he expected to live out his days in New England, but after World War I, "my thoughts turned to the uncivilized West." He moved to Rincon Point, farmed on the ranch, nearly went broke, and got a job selling real estate in Santa Paula.

His youngest brother, Edward Holland Bates, joined him in California after college in 1925. The two of them bought additional Rincon Point beachfront. Edward built the first house on the new tract, graded roads, and constructed a bridge across Rincon Creek. Over the next half century, the two brothers transformed Rincon Point. To the end of their long lives—Robert died at 90, Edward at almost 99—they still considered the place extraordinary.

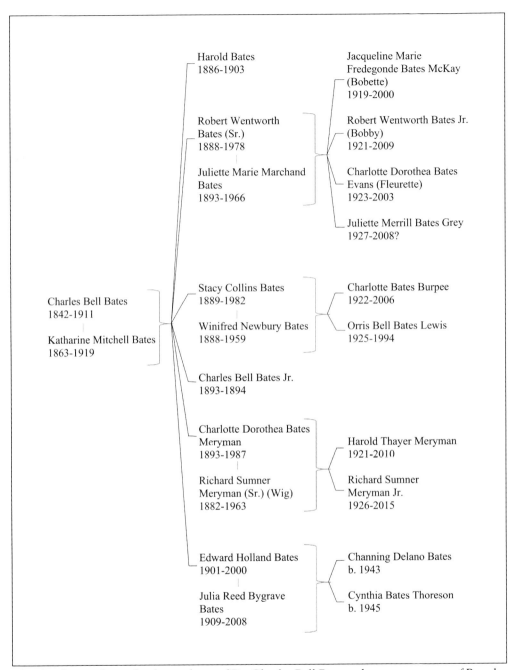

Harold Bates
1886-1903

Jacqueline Marie
Fredegonde Bates McKay
(Bobette)
1919-2000

Robert Wentworth
Bates (Sr.)
1888-1978

Robert Wentworth Bates Jr.
(Bobby)
1921-2009

Juliette Marie Marchand
Bates
1893-1966

Charlotte Dorothea Bates
Evans (Fleurette)
1923-2003

Juliette Merrill Bates Grey
1927-2008?

Charles Bell Bates
1842-1911

Katharine Mitchell Bates
1863-1919

Stacy Collins Bates
1889-1982

Charlotte Bates Burpee
1922-2006

Winifred Newbury Bates
1888-1959

Orris Bell Bates Lewis
1925-1994

Charles Bell Bates Jr.
1893-1894

Charlotte Dorothea Bates
Meryman
1893-1987

Harold Thayer Meryman
1921-2010

Richard Sumner
Meryman (Sr.) (Wig)
1882-1963

Richard Sumner
Meryman Jr.
1926-2015

Edward Holland Bates
1901-2000

Channing Delano Bates
b. 1943

Julia Reed Bygrave
Bates
1909-2008

Cynthia Bates Thoreson
b. 1945

This family tree shows the descendants of Dr. Charles Bell Bates, who was an owner of Rancho El Rincon starting in 1885. Dr. Bates's son Robert W. Bates Sr. built one of the first cottages on the point. Another son, Edward, partnered with Robert to buy beachfront west of Rincon Creek from the Hill family in the late 1920s. Edward built the first house on the new tract in about 1929. Dr. Bates's other children, Stacy C. Bates and Dorothea Bates Meryman, also owned property on the point but mostly lived elsewhere. (Courtesy Bates family.)

Dr. Charles Bell Bates poses around 1889 with his son Harold and family dog Nero. Born in Leeds, England, Bates came to the United States in 1860, age 18, to help his stockbroker father manage a water project. He subsequently attended Toland Medical College in San Francisco. In 1869, he established a practice in Santa Barbara in partnership with Mateo Henry Biggs, a self-taught physician from Peru who owned Rancho El Rincon. (With Bates's encouragement, Biggs got a medical degree.) In 1885, Bates and pharmacist Benigno Gutierrez each put up $5,000 to buy Biggs's remaining holdings in the Rincon ranch, roughly 2,000 acres. When, around 1902, Bates discovered a more lucrative opportunity—a Boston company that sold pianos on installment, with buyers paying 12-percent interest—he liquidated most of his Santa Barbara holdings, moved to Cambridge, and put his money into what became the Bates-Mitchell Piano Co. He listed his share of the Rincon ranch for sale at $25,000, according to his son Edward. It would have been a tidy profit on his $5,000 investment two decades earlier, but there were no takers. (Courtesy Bates family.)

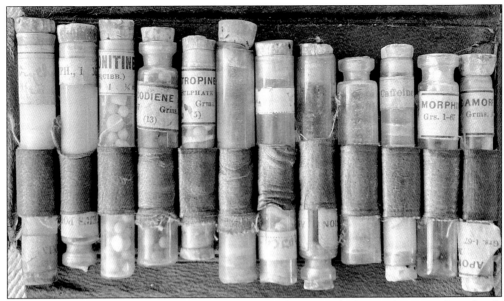

Dr. Bates carried these vials of codeine, morphine, strychnine, and other medications. Seated with ramrod-straight posture, he often rode through Santa Barbara on a bicycle, wearing a dark suit and a bowler with his shoes freshly shined. When one little boy asked his mother where babies come from, she said that Dr. Bates brought them in his bicycle basket. (Courtesy Bates family.)

In 1885, Dr. Bates married an English-born schoolteacher raised in Massachusetts, Katharine Mitchell. She was 22; he was 43. In 1903, their oldest child, 17-year-old Harold, drowned while vacationing in Maine. Katharine never recovered, according to her youngest son, Edward. She rarely laughed, and suffering from anxiety, she often kept a pistol within reach. She hired a series of mediums in hopes of contacting Harold in the spirit world. (Courtesy Bates family.)

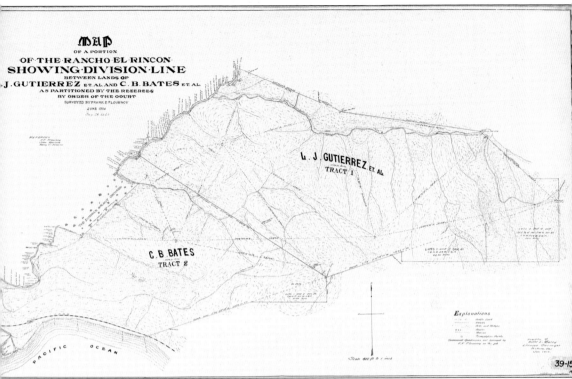

Benigno Gutierrez, who co-owned Rancho El Rincon with Charles Bell Bates, died in 1902. His family seems to have run into financial hardship thereafter. In 1904, they sold the Gutierrez Drugstore in Santa Barbara. In 1905, they sued to dissolve the Rancho El Rincon partnership with Dr. Bates, perhaps in order to mortgage their share. A Ventura County judge appointed three referees to divide the ranch into two tracts of equal value. (One of them was John Bailard, whose father, Andrew, had bought about 400 acres of Rancho El Rincon from Dr. Biggs in 1868.) Dr. Bates, according to his grandson Bobby, got first choice, and he took the smaller tract, about 755 acres extending to the shore. The Gutierrez family got a 1,233-acre tract that was more mountainous and remote. (Courtesy Ventura County Superior Court.)

The member of the Bates family who had the greatest impact on Rincon Point was Charles and Katharine's son Robert Wentworth Bates Sr. He grew up in Santa Barbara, graduated from Harvard, and went to work for the family's Bates-Mitchell Piano Co. in Boston. Hungry for adventure, he volunteered to drive an ambulance in World War I. He ultimately headed the Red Cross ambulance service in Italy. (One of the men under his command, Lt. Ernest Hemingway, wrote about "what a shit Capt. Bates was," though he also named one of his cats Bates.) In this photograph from about 1919, Bates poses for a portrait painted by a war buddy, Richard Sumner Meryman, known as Wig. After the war, Bates opted to become a gentleman farmer on his family's portion of Rancho El Rincon, which he named Rincon del Mar. (Courtesy Bates family.)

Juliette Marchand was a nurse at the American Hospital in Paris. During the war, Robert W. Bates was treated there for appendicitis. He proposed, she accepted, and they married in Paris on New Year's Eve of 1918 and sailed for America. In Santa Barbara, Edward Bates, 17, never forgot his first encounter with Juliette. "My new little brother," she said, and kissed him on the lips. (Courtesy Bates family.)

After Charles and Katharine Bates died, Robert W. Bates owned the Rincon ranch in partnership with his three siblings—from left to right in this photograph from about 1924, Dorothea Bates Meryman, Edward Holland Bates, and Stacy Collins Bates—plus their uncle Harry Mitchell. After the war, when Robert announced his plans to raise crops on the Bates ranch, Stacy remarked that he had no evident qualifications other than his surname. (Courtesy Bates family.)

Robert W. Bates poses at Rincon Point in 1920 with his wife, Juliette, and their first child, Bobette, plus fox terrier Monty. Bates's crops (lima beans and hay) failed, and he was forced to acknowledge, in his words, that "a gentleman's C in college and knowing one's way about Paris, however worthy in themselves, are poor qualifications for a rancher." He recruited Japanese farmer Kijuro Ota to take over. (Courtesy Bates family.)

On first arriving at Rincon Point in 1919, Robert W. Bates rented a cottage from the Hill family. Around 1922, he spent $400, in his recollection, to build this board-and-batten cottage on a Rincon Creek estuary. Soon thereafter, the family moved to Santa Paula, where he got a job selling real estate, and the beach cottage became a weekend getaway. (Courtesy Bates family.)

Through a window of their cottage, Robert W. Bates photographed his wife, Juliette, playing with one of their children. A Rincon Creek flood in April 1926 damaged the structure, and Bates had it dragged to a safer location. According to his daughter Bobette, he moved it two more times in the next few years, farther and farther away from the creek. (Courtesy Bates family.)

Robert W. Bates took pride in his frugality. He fined his children a penny each time they left a light on, ground wheat by hand and boiled it as a cheap substitute for oatmeal, and bought tools to resole shoes at home. Here, he proudly displays a tub he found in a junkyard. When he discovered a bargain, according to one acquaintance, his face glowed with a sort of religious ecstasy. (Courtesy Bates family.)

Katharine Bates's English-born brother Harry Mitchell was a co-owner of Rancho El Rincon. He settled in Santa Barbara in the 1880s and worked for the Gutierrez Drugstore. Around 1900, he moved to Boston and helped run what became the Bates-Mitchell Piano Co., where Robert Bates photographed him in 1909. Opinionated and irascible, Mitchell decreed that the company would not advertise, because ads were a waste of money, and it would not sell the Edison phonograph, because it was a flash-in-the-pan fad. A trade magazine dryly observed that Bates-Mitchell's business volume "has not been such as to make expansion necessary." When the company failed, Mitchell returned to California and built the cottage shown below, its walls lined with books. The 1926 flood inflicted major damage. According to Bobette Bates, books washed up on the beach for months. (Both, courtesy Bates family.)

The three older Bates children stand by their Rincon Point beach cottage. They are, from left to right, Jacqueline Marie Fredegonde Bates, known as Bobette; Charlotte Dorothea Bates, known as Fleurette, and Robert Wentworth Bates Jr., known as Bobby. The children grew up, in Bobby's recollection, "running free and unsupervised." (Courtesy Bates family.)

On a nearly empty Rincon Point, Robert W. Bates photographs his fourth child, Juliette Merrill Bates, while Ruth Jerrard, who worked for the family, stands by. Bates frequently took photographs and movies of Rincon Point floods, bonfires, boat launchings, and holiday celebrations. (Courtesy Bates family.)

During the Depression, much of the farming on the Rincon ranch came to a temporary halt. Horses were put out to pasture, and cropland gave way to mustard and thistle. In 1935, Robert W. Bates allowed his son Bobby, who was 14 at the time, to farm around 15 acres of the idle land. In Bobby's recollection, he hired a laborer named Waldo Ramirez for $2.25 a day. He would get Ramirez started every morning, attend school in Carpinteria, and return to supervise. The first year's hay crop was a disappointment, but the following year, with the help of Kenji Ota and Fernando Ramirez (Waldo's brother), he made several hundred dollars from lima beans. According to Bobby, his father then sent him away to boarding school in hopes that he would develop loftier ambitions than dirt farming. This photograph shows Bobby in 1938 at Midland School in Los Olivos. (Courtesy Bates family.)

In 1936, Bobby Bates organized the Rincon Handicap Horse Races Bates Sweepstakes on Rincon Point. Entrants paid 25¢ to compete. In this photograph, Joan Rock leads, followed by Benny Baker, Lawry Bailard, Bobby Bates, and Jerry Rubel. (Courtesy Bates family.)

Diminutive Joan Rock, who was not quite 11 years old, won the Rincon race. "She claims her horse was really fast," wrote one of the riders she defeated, Lawry Bailard, "but I maintain that he didn't have to carry much and should have been handicapped." In 1994, when they were both about 70, Bailard and Rock set aside any lingering bitterness over the 1936 race and got married. (Courtesy Bates family.)

49

In 1937, sixteen-year-old Bobby Bates owned two Model Ts, both barely functioning. This photograph shows one of his many automotive misadventures. His cousin Harry Meryman (left), Bates (right), and two unidentified companions push a Model T through the surf between Carpinteria and Rincon Point. (Courtesy Meryman family.)

Bobby Bates's second Model T was this pickup. He and Harry Meryman installed dual tires on the back so that they could drive through orchards. They also added rear seats, occupied here by Minoru Ota and dog Ritzy. When the car was carrying a full load of passengers, however, the front wheels sometimes left the ground. There were other problems too, as the sign indicates. (Courtesy Bates family.)

Edward Holland Bates, shown here about 1919 with his brother Robert's car and family dog Monty, was the youngest of Charles Bell Bates's children. He was born in 1901 in Cambridge, Massachusetts, eight years after his sister Dorothea. ("Whether I was a blessing or a mistake," he said, "in my own estimation, I'm glad it happened.") Edward studied at Harvard and returned to the West. In the late 1920s, he partnered with his brother Robert to buy several additional acres of Rincon Point beachfront in Santa Barbara County for about $25,000. The sellers were the family of the late rancher-physician Reuben W. Hill. Edward spent years as foreman of the family's Rincon del Mar Ranch. In addition to farming, he planted trees, installed pipelines, and graded roads at Rincon Point. (Courtesy Bates family.)

In about 1929, Edward Bates built the first house on the new Bates property on the west side of Rincon Creek—a cottage with redwood walls and a solid oak floor, nestled by a big Monterey cypress. He learned to install wiring and plumbing from the Sears catalog. The cottage cost $3,163.66. His nephew Bobby Bates took this photograph in about 1934. (Courtesy Bates family.)

In about 1934, Edward Bates met Julia Bygrave, a Radcliffe graduate from Concord, Massachusetts, who was teaching at the Ojai Valley School. They married in 1936. This photograph shows them in their Rincon Point cottage. They lived there until the 1950s, when they moved to Santa Barbara. (Courtesy Biddle/Boyle family.)

In the above photograph from the 1930s, Bates family dog Monty sits by the then-impassable road across Rincon Creek. To reach his house by car, Edward Bates first laid planks across the creek bed, but he forgot to remove them and a storm washed them out to sea. Next he jury-rigged a bridge, largely from lumber found on the beach, but it started to collapse under a milk truck and had to be abandoned. When buyers of lots on the west side of the creek asked, not unreasonably, for a safe way to reach their property, Edward enlisted a Hollywood artist to design a two-way steel bridge with stone columns. His brother Robert wanted a bare-bones one-way wooden bridge. (Edward's wardrobe came from Beverly Hills; Robert's came from thrift stores.) They compromised on the two-way wooden bridge shown below. Completed in 1940, it lasted until 1973. (Above, courtesy Bates family; below, courtesy Biddle/Boyle family.)

In 1956, the Bates family picnics beneath a *palapa* at Rincon Point. Wig Meryman is at left, in bowtie. In hats, their backs to the camera, are Edward Bates (left) and Robert Bates. Harry Meryman is at right, near his wife, Lanie, both wearing sunglasses. Across the table, the woman drinking is probably Julia Bates. She is seated next to Dick Meryman, who is inflating something for the children. (Courtesy Meryman family.)

Robert and Juliette Bates's youngest child, also named Juliette, married David Grey, a physician, and they built a house near the tip of Rincon Point in the late 1950s. This 1959 Christmas gathering at the Greys' features, from left to right, Wig and Dorothea Meryman, Julia and Cynthia Bates, Juliette and David Grey, and Edward Bates. (Cynthia is Edward and Julia's daughter.) (Courtesy Bates family.)

Harry and Lanie Meryman stand by a jeep at Rincon Point in the 1950s. The child is unidentified. (Courtesy Meryman family.)

The Bates family was indebted to the Ramirez family. Fernando Ramirez, shown here, spent his career as Rincon ranch foreman, including projects at Rincon Point. His sister Antonia worked from her teens until retirement in Robert Bates's household as cook, housekeeper, and nanny. Their brother Waldo plowed land for teenage farmer Bobby Bates and graded Rincon Point roads. (Courtesy Pat Ramirez Saragosa.)

Robert W. Bates, shown here in the late 1960s, considered the Rincon ranch one of the treasures of the California coast. "Who will be living on our lands 100 years hence?" he wrote. "We do not know, but we do know that for the few brief years that they are ours, we can preserve them for others to enjoy for unnumbered years to come." He died in 1978, age 90. (Courtesy Robbie Hutto.)

Siblings Bobette McKay, Bobby Bates, Juliette Grey, and Fleurette Evans reunite at Rincon Point in 1962. Bobette died in 2000, Fleurette died in 2003, and Bobby died in 2009. In about 1979, Juliette moved to her late father's house. Suffering from dementia, she disappeared in 2003 and was declared dead in 2008. The last to live at the point was Bobette, who got a house there around 1975. When she died, the family's 115-year association with Rincon Point came to an end. (Courtesy Bates family.)

Five

A Japanese Farmer

Rincon Point was desolate at the beginning of the 20th century and opulent at the end. For a few years in between, it was verdant and productive, thanks to Japanese sharecropper Kijuro Ota.

Robert W. Bates, whose family owned the Rincon ranch, invited Ota to raise crops there in 1922 in exchange for housing and a share of the profits. Ota moved his wife and six children into a beach cottage, close to the cottage occupied by Bates, his wife, and two children. (Two more Ota children and two more Bates children came later.) Ota's first crop, cantaloupe, proved successful, and Bates had him expand to other parts of the ranch. Meanwhile, their children became fast friends, especially Kenji Ota and Bobby Bates.

Robert Bates terminated the sharecropper arrangement during the Depression, which proved to be a propitious development for the Otas. They started their own farming enterprise, K. Ota & Sons, and sold produce to wholesalers in Los Angeles. No longer did the Otas work for the Bateses. In summer 1941, after his freshman year at Harvard, Bobby Bates worked for the Otas.

But after Pearl Harbor, American officials feared that people of Japanese descent on the West Coast would commit sabotage, so the Army took them into custody and moved them inland. In 1942, most members of the Ota family were sent to a processing center in the San Joaquin Valley and then to a camp in Arizona. Robert Bates considered the relocation program a travesty. He looked after the Otas' crops and livestock in their absence.

The Otas returned in 1945. Unlike many other West Coast farmers of Japanese descent, they still owned their property (their descendants still do), and they were able to revive their business, but they never matched their prewar success.

This chapter relies on oral history interviews with members of the Ota family, edited by Jim Campos and published in *Grapevine*, the newsletter of the Carpinteria Valley Museum of History, in 2020 and 2021.

Kijuro Ota, at right in this photograph from the late 1920s, left his home in Niigata, Japan, in 1903, age 19, and immigrated to the United States. He found work first as a house servant and then as a farmhand. In 1912, friends of the Ota family in Japan, the Sakais, sent their daughter Hideko—at left here, holding their son, Minoru, who was born in 1926—to California to be Kijuro's bride in an arranged marriage. In 1922, when Kijuro was working on a farm in Bardsdale in Ventura County, he met Robert W. Bates, one of the owners of the Rincon del Mar Ranch. Bates had raised crops on the ranch but could not make it pay. He was looking for someone to take over in exchange for housing and a share of the profits. Kijuro Ota inspected the property and agreed. (Courtesy Ota family.)

Kijuro Ota cultivated a field near the beach at Rincon Point with a horse-drawn plow and planted cantaloupe. Robert W. Bates told him to irrigate from a lagoon fed by Rincon Creek, but it proved to be too briny because of ocean backwash, so he apparently watered the new plantings once with buckets and then raised them without water. Bates judged the cantaloupe delicious and the crop yield remarkable, and he invited Ota to expand to other parts of the Rincon ranch. Ota's crops are at left in this 1920s photograph. Note the creek in the back and, precariously close to it, the beach house and outbuilding, probably the Bates family's; the Merryland Inn at right, repeatedly raided during Prohibition; and the hay wagon passing the hotel. (Courtesy Ota family.)

The five Ota girls pose in 1927. From left to right, Miyeko and Sumiye are in back, and Hanaye, Kazuye, and Masaye are in front. In addition to the five daughters, the Otas had three sons, Kenji, Minoru, and Toshikazu, who went by Tom. All eight were born at home. In their early years living at Rincon Point, some of the children attended a one-room school at Punta Gorda (now La Conchita), about two miles east of the point. To get there, they walked on the beach at low tide, but at high tide, they had to walk along the railroad tracks or on the edge of the coast highway's wooden causeways. Some of the 12-inch causeway planks stopped short of the edge, leaving gaps. Once when the Ota children were walking to school with children from the Ramirez family, who lived nearby, Sumiye tumbled through an opening and landed on the beach below, embarrassed but unhurt. (Courtesy Ota family.)

From left to right, Masaye, Kazuye, and Hanaye Ota sit in a go-cart built by their mechanically minded brother Kenji, who was always at work on some project. (Courtesy Bates family.)

In the mid-1920s, three children wade in the Pacific at Rincon Point, probably Bobby Bates, Kazuye Ota, and Bobette Bates. Bobette and Kazuye were close friends. In an oral history interview for the Carpinteria Valley Museum of History, Bobette remembered sitting on a sand dune with Kazuye and chanting, "Doodle bug, doodle bug," until one appeared. She thought it was magic. (Courtesy Bates family.)

In this photograph from the mid-1920s, from left to right, Kenji Ota takes Bobby and Bobette Bates sailing. The children sometimes overloaded and capsized the raft, according to Sumiye, which was risky because not all of the Ota children could swim. (Courtesy Bates family.)

In about 1935, from left to right, Fleurette Bates and Masaye, Hanaye, and Minoru Ota return from school. After the birth of Minoru, the eighth (and final) child, the Otas moved from the beach to a bigger house, also owned by the Bates family. (Courtesy Ota family.)

Kenji Ota and Bobby Bates sit by a playhouse in the mid-1920s. Like the Ota children, Bobby called Kijuro and Hideko Ota *otoosan* and *okaasan*—Japanese for mother and father. On one occasion, he and Kenji wrenched the plug out of an abandoned oilwell on Rincon Point and tried to peer down the hole. For illumination, Kenji lit a wooden match. It ignited an explosion and a column of fire that sent them both flying. Kenji got the worst of it; the flames burned off his eyelashes and eyebrows, singed his face, and temporarily blinded him. "I had to lead him home," Bobby recounted in 1999, "where his long-suffering mother smeared Crisco all over his puffy face. . . . It is a real wonder that we survived our childhood." (Courtesy Bates family.)

In 1934, Robert W. Bates ended the sharecropper arrangement with Kijuro Ota because he needed the irrigation water for lemon orchards on the Rincon ranch. Ota concentrated on raising crops on his own farm in Carpinteria and on farmland he leased in Santa Barbara and Ventura Counties. He began marketing produce under the label K. Ota & Sons. (Courtesy Ota family.)

K. Ota & Sons prospered, and soon, the Otas were able to buy a new tractor, shown here with Tom at the wheel. Tom marketed their produce to several wholesale outlets in Los Angeles. They continued to farm until 1942, when the federal government sent Japanese and Japanese Americans on the West Coast to internment camps. (Courtesy Ota family.)

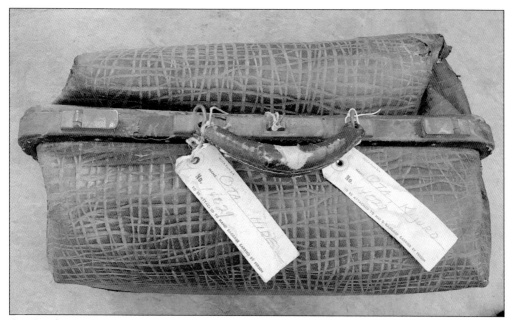

On April 30, 1942, not quite five months after Pearl Harbor, the Otas had to leave their home near Rincon Point. From Santa Barbara, they traveled by train to a processing center in Tulare, California, a 10-hour journey. They were allowed to take only what they could carry. This is Hideko Ota's satchel. (Courtesy Ota family.)

Except for one married daughter, the Otas were sent to the Tulare processing center and then to this camp in Gila River, Arizona. The Bates family took care of their property and visited them in the camps. When internees were allowed to take jobs (but not on the West Coast), Kijuro Ota worked in New Jersey making boxes for shipping fruit, and Tom and Kenji worked for a Chicago trucking company. (Courtesy Ota family.)

This prewar photograph shows K. Ota and sons, from left to right, Kenji, Kijuro, Minoru, and Tom. When the family departed for internment in 1942, Mrs. Ota expected to be away for a few months. It proved to be three years. Although they resumed farming in 1945, they never matched their earlier success. Tom was convinced that the relocation program was driven by economics. He believed—and some historians agree—that rather than protecting the coastline from saboteurs, the program was implemented for the sake of protecting Caucasian farmers from competition. In 1942, when the Otas were giving away some of their belongings before leaving for internment, Tom said they might as well get rid of their American flag, as it no longer truly belonged to them. Kenji said no, it was the flag he had been born under, and he wanted to keep it. (Courtesy Ota family.)

Six

RINCON ON CANVAS

Many artists have sought to capture Rincon Point on canvas, but for duration and depth, nobody rivals Richard Sumner Meryman (1882–1963), who painted scenes on the point from the 1920s to the 1960s.

Wig Meryman, as he was known, was born in Boston and studied at the Museum School of Fine Arts. He worked as a copyist for Abbott Thayer and contributed to Thayer's book *Concealing Coloration in the Animal Kingdom*, published in 1909, a pioneering attempt to identify the principles of natural camouflage. In 1916, the Guild of Boston Artists held an exhibition of Meryman's paintings, which one critic called the best show of the year. The eminent painter John Singer Sargent praised his work too.

Meryman volunteered for the ambulance service in World War I—partly, according to his son Dick, to get away from an unhappy romance—and became a lieutenant in the Camouflage Corps when the United States entered the war. In 1919, he visited a friend from the ambulance service, Robert W. Bates, at the Rincon ranch. He met Bates's sister Dorothea, and they married later that year. They moved to Washington, DC, where Meryman started a job as assistant principal of the Corcoran School of Art. In 1926, he was promoted to principal. Although the Merymans lived in the East, they spent many summers at the Rincon ranch, crossing the country by car or train with their sons Harry and Dick. Robert Bates converted an old garage into an artist's studio.

Meryman despised modern art, a view that placed him at odds with the artistic establishment. He left the Corcoran School in 1935 and moved to Dublin, New Hampshire. Although he largely refused to work with galleries or art dealers, his paintings are in the collections of the Corcoran Gallery of Art, the Smithsonian American Art Museum, Georgetown University, Phillips Andover Academy, and the New Hampshire State House.

Wig Meryman had no patience for theorizing about art or the artistic process. On the beach at Rincon Point, he once suggested that his son Harry, a medical researcher, try painting a watercolor landscape. Harry asked, "How?" "Draw the picture," Wig replied, "and then color it."

In 1919, Dorothea Bates clowns around at Rincon Point with her fiancé, Richard S. Meryman, known as Wig. They married in Carpinteria in June and moved to Washington, DC, where Meryman had been hired as assistant principal of the Corcoran School of Art. In 1926, he was promoted to principal. During this period, modernism cleaved the art world. Some modernists dismissed realist art as humdrum and mechanical, whereas some realists dismissed modernism as gimmicky and pretentious. Wig Meryman was in the latter camp. In 1923, students at the Pennsylvania Academy of Fine Arts petitioned to have him removed from the classroom (he was a part-time instructor) because of his opposition to modern art. He survived that uprising, but in 1935, a modernist claque pushed him out of the Corcoran School. The Merymans moved to Dublin, New Hampshire. (Courtesy Meryman family.)

In this self-portrait, Wig Meryman roars with laughter at modernists for considering themselves the equals of classical artists; the latter are represented by the Renaissance-style figures in the background. He refused to work with gallerists or dealers, whom he blamed for the dominance of modern art. The biggest exhibition of his works was held not in a gallery or a museum but in a New Hampshire barn. (Courtesy Meryman family.)

Painted in 1922, Wig Meryman's portrait of his wife, Dorothea, appeared in a show at the Pennsylvania Academy of Fine Arts in 1923. Along with landscapes of California and New Hampshire, he painted portraits of many military leaders, university presidents, and government officials. Critics praised his work, though some noted that his traditionalist approach was out of step with the times. (Courtesy Meryman family.)

Above, Wig Meryman works on a Rincon Point landscape in the early 1930s while sitting by Edward Bates's cottage. Meryman produced a series of paintings from that vantage point, including the one below. The two-toned house in the painting belonged to Edwin Ardell Hill. (Above, courtesy Meryman family; below, courtesy Burpee family.)

This painting by Wig Meryman is thought to depict one of the first cottages on Rincon Point, which Robert W. Bates built in the early 1920s next to the mouth of Rincon Creek. Because of floods, Bates moved the cottage away from the creek several times. Meryman probably painted it in one of its later, drier sites. (Courtesy Meryman family.)

Edward H. Bates designed and built a bridge over Rincon Creek in the late 1930s, and owned this painting of it by Wig Meryman. (Courtesy Cynthia Bates Thoreson.)

In 1962, the year before he died, Wig Meryman painted this landscape of an empty lot just west of the tip of the Rincon Point, adjacent to the house then occupied by Juliette Bates Grey and her husband, David. Robert W. Bates Jr., known in the family as Bobby, owned both the painting and the property. (Courtesy Bates family.)

In about 1960, Wig and Dorothea Meryman built a house on Puesta del Sol on Rincon Point. Wig probably painted this landscape from their patio or one of the adjoining ones. After he died in 1963, Dorothea spent more time at Rincon Point, finally leaving New Hampshire to live there full-time in about 1980. She died in 1987. (Courtesy Pat Ramirez Saragosa.)

Seven

TRANSPORTATION AND BUSINESS

Before the Rincon Point area became a famous destination, it was an infamous obstacle. In the mid-19th century, some called it the greatest impediment to travel between San Francisco and San Diego. Just east of the point, the beach ended in a steep cliff, and sand was the only path for horses, wagons, and, later, automobiles. It was often impassable at high tide. Even at low tide, travelers had to navigate around obstacles that fell from the bluffs or washed up from the sea. In 1872, when the legislature created Ventura County out of the eastern portion of Santa Barbara County, with Rincon Creek as the dividing line, Rincon Point was a major reason. It was too hard for residents of San Buenaventura, as Ventura was then known, to reach the county seat of Santa Barbara.

Transportation had other impacts as well. Farmers east of the point had trouble hauling produce over the beach to Santa Barbara, which meant they could not ship it to San Francisco. Some boosters envisioned Santa Barbara as a health resort and tourist destination, but only if people could get there. In 1878, an alternative route opened, the Casitas Pass road, but in places, it was narrow and steep, and floods and landslides sometimes blocked it. According to local historian Walker Tompkins, the pace of progress in Santa Barbara depended, to a substantial extent, on the state of transportation around Rincon Point.

Transportation influenced development at Rincon Point too. After the wooden causeways in 1912 made it easier (though still not easy) to reach the point, a hotel opened with a restaurant, a bar, and an unsavory reputation. By the 1950s, Robert W. Bates was promoting Rincon Point as an easy commute from Ventura. Good roads, as the *Santa Barbara Gazette* said in 1857, are "a never-failing source of prosperity."

In the 1860s, artist Edward Vischer was aboard a stagecoach trapped by the tide near Rincon Point. The driver maneuvered next to the cliff to wait for low tide. The surf battered the horses, and the coach tipped 45 degrees. Vischer loved it. He later drew this sketch. (If he misread the topography, blame it on his narrow view through the stagecoach window.) (Courtesy Huntington Library.)

THE ASPHALTUM-REGION.   Dᴿ BIGGS' RANCHO „ RINCON

Edward Vischer also drew this sketch of a stagecoach descending toward the station on Rincon Creek, close to Rincon Point. Vischer wrote that Rancho El Rincon, with its "fine groves of oaks and sycamores to the very mouth of the creek," was "one of the most romantic spots" he had seen in California. (Courtesy Bancroft Library, University of California, Berkeley.)

Southern Pacific surveyors set up these tents near Rincon Point in 1887. When it came time to lay track later that year, a much bigger encampment sprang up: 250 tents, 8 kitchens, 4 cobblers, 2 illicit saloons, and more than a thousand laborers. (Museum of Ventura County.)

Between Santa Barbara and Ventura, the Southern Pacific made several stops early in the 20th century: Montecito, Summerland, Miramar, and Benham at Rincon Point. In this undated photograph of Benham, Maria Del Carmen Hill, widow of Dr. Reuben Hill and matriarch of the Hill family, is at right. The railroad abandoned the Benham stop in 1940. (Courtesy Suzanne Rhodes.)

In a 1903 derailment, two Southern Pacific cars tumbled 35 feet onto the beach near Rincon Point, and another caught on a ledge part way down. It was the subject of many newspaper articles and illustrations, including this sketch of the tumbled cars and a man who was injured. Miraculously, no one was killed. (Courtesy *San Francisco Examiner*.)

"Quite a large piece of my Rincon Ranch has dropped into the Pacific Ocean," Charles Bell Bates told his family in 1909, "taking with it a locomotive, three cars and three men, who are still buried under tons of earth." Actually, the avalanche buried alive four railroad workers. Recovering the bodies took five weeks. (Courtesy Doug Treloar.)

Railroad watchman Cipriano Ramirez, shown at right, was born in Mexico and got a job with the Southern Pacific in El Paso. In 1911, the railroad transferred him to Carpinteria and sent him, his wife, and their two children there by boxcar. According to his grandson Joe Velasquez Jr., Ramirez was responsible for 10 miles of track in Ventura County, which included Rincon Point. Landslides from the cliffs were frequent. When there was too much rubble for Ramirez to clear, he would place blasting caps on the rails, and the explosions would signal the engineer to stop the train. The photograph below shows Ramirez's son Fernando with a wagon in front of what is probably a boxcar for train workers. On the flatcar behind it, note the proto-Porta Potty. (Both, courtesy Ramirez family.)

According to roadbuilder R.G. Percy, Ventura County owned the right-of-way for a route around Rincon but deeded it to the Southern Pacific because, at the time, the train was thought to be the final stage in transportation's evolution. When automobiles became popular a few years later, engineers found that the railroad had taken the only practical path. (Courtesy Carpinteria Valley Museum of History.)

Where the beach abutted the rocky embankment near Rincon Point, high tide could trap a car just as it had trapped stagecoaches. In the 1920s, when this photograph was taken, most motorists avoided the peril by driving over wooden causeways. This driver took the road less traveled and had cause to regret it. Rincon Point is in the background. (Courtesy Atchison [Otto] Collection, Gledhill Library, Santa Barbara Historical Museum.)

In 1912, Rincon passage became easier thanks to the opening of three causeways over parts of the beach, with a foot-deep clay road laid over the sand between them. Private funds paid for most of the project. Milo M. Potter of the Potter Hotel in Santa Barbara solicited money from his fellow hoteliers up and down the coast. Additional funds came from dances, parades, car washes, and a minstrel show. When the road was finished, a hundred-car caravan drove from Los Angeles to Santa Barbara and back over it. Unfortunately, the heavy traffic shredded the clay surface between causeways and required substantial repairs. In this famous photograph, drivers from the Inyo Good Road Club display their Studebakers on one of the causeways, with Rincon Point in the background. (Courtesy California Department of Transportation Library.)

Clarence Cadwell of Carpinteria poses at the wheel with his dog. In traffic, the causeways rattled and swayed, especially when drivers exceeded the speed limit, generally 15 miles per hour. Before the wooden surface was paved in 1916, nails often came loose and punctured tires. (Courtesy John Rodriguez.)

Between 1925 and 1927, the state replaced the causeways with a road on landfill protected by a seawall. Ornamental stairways descended to the beach. Then as now, construction impeded traffic and irritated drivers. In September 1927, the *Ventura County Star* reported that it would soon be possible, for the first time in two and a half years, to drive from Ventura to Santa Barbara without any construction detours or delays. (Courtesy Santa Barbara Historical Museum.)

This photograph from the late 1940s shows the two-lane highway at the intersection of Bates Road. In 1944, Ventura County put up a sign naming the road after a Carpinteria judge who had farmed nearby, Jerome F. Tubbs. Robert W. Bates, whose ranch and house were located on the road, called a county official and complained that Tubbs Road was a dreadful name. The official proposed Bates Road as an alternative. Bates said that sounded fine. (Courtesy Meryman family.)

Starting in the late 1960s, Caltrans widened US 101 at Rincon Point. This 1970 photograph shows the magnitude of the project. Workers removed some five million cubic yards of dirt and rock just above Rincon Point, by the Bates Road exit, and used it to fashion a new mesa inside the adjacent canyon. (Courtesy California Department of Transportation Library.)

Men drill for oil around 1920 on Rincon Point, west of the creek mouth. The Rincon area had long been popular with oil prospectors. In 1864, chemist Benjamin Silliman Jr. of Yale University said that "Biggs's Place"—Rancho El Rincon—had the earmarks of a major oil deposit, including tar seepages near the beach, "offensive gases" emanating from the so-called volcano on the hillside, and "one of the most surprising and beautiful sights in nature"—an oil-slick rainbow that was occasionally visible on the surface of the sea. Near the site of the drilling shown here, one and sometimes two derrick towers appear in photographs taken a few years later, but the oil evidently dried up. In the late 1920s, Edward H. Bates used one of the old derricks for a massive bonfire. (Courtesy Bates family.)

In 1915, Burt O. Clark opened the Hotel Rincon (above, with separate cabins seen below). His wife, Ruby, helped run it, spawning the nickname Aunt Ruby's Roadhouse. (Ruby was a daughter of the late Dr. Reuben Hill.) In 1916, Santa Barbara clergy condemned the Clarks for serving alcohol to minors, employing a 14-year-old girl as an "exhibition dancer," and tolerating unspecified "immoral conduct" on the veranda. When the Clarks could not get the liquor license required under a new law, they left town. Under different names—including the Rincon Inn, Carl's, and, in this photograph from about 1924, the Merryland Inn—and different managers, the place became a notorious honky-tonk during Prohibition. According to local lore, managers and customers could evade arrest because the county line passed through the bar, so that when Santa Barbara County police raided it, everyone would run to the Ventura County side, and vice-versa. That tale appears to be fiction. In fact, hotel manager Harry Goldflam was arrested and jailed in 1920, during the first year of Prohibition. (Both, courtesy Bates family.)

Behind Rincon Point, on property owned by L.L. Brentner, a brickyard began operating in 1921. It produced bricks of yellow and other pastel hues owing to clay in the soil. The yard apparently closed in the 1930s, but bricks continued washing up on the beach after storms for decades. Pictured is what remained of the kiln in the 1960s, shortly before US 101 expansion buried it. (Courtesy Carpinteria Valley Museum of History.)

Welcome to Arrow Beach (later re-released as *Tender Flesh*) is a 1974 slasher movie partly filmed at Rincon Point. In it, a sheriff and deputy watch a woman approach the bridge shown here. The sheriff says she will soon be trespassing. No, says the deputy, not if she stays on the beach. "One thing you've got to learn, chum," the sheriff replies. "Private property owners don't see it that way." Scenes of cannibalism and incest follow. (Courtesy Laurence Harvey Productions.)

Eight

SURFING RINCON

Due to favorable topography and seasonal swells, the winter surf at Rincon Point is legendary. For 75 years, the famous right-breaking beach with long winter waves has lured the best surfers, as well as nurtured generations of local stars. It has also served as an open-air laboratory for many of the sport's key innovators. The Rincon "brand" is famous, synonymous with a laid-back yet deep commitment to riding perfect waves away from the hubbub and kooks down south. This commitment is best represented by Renny Yater, who hung up his shaping shingle locally in 1959 and never looked back. Or by Kemp Aaberg's iconic soul arch at Rincon (also 1959), which became *Surfer* magazine's logo, for proof of the pure joy found in Rincon's waves.

Paying respect to the queen was and is mandatory in surfing circles. In fact, one is not a surfer if he or she has not ridden Rincon. Miki Dora surfed here, Greg Noll, Phil Edwards, Mickey Munoz, Kemp and Denny Aaberg, David Nuuhiwa, Al Merrick, Kim Mearig, Tom Curren, Lakey Peterson, and on and on. As did famous Aussies like Nat Young, who came away transformed by the experience. And one cannot forget the pioneers—Mike Sturmer and Gates Foss prewar, and Joe Quigg, Mondos Mary, and the great waterman Billy Meng postwar.

Rincon has its own greatest generation with the Carpinteria High School class of 1967, which overflowed with talent. It even has its greatest wave, a monster that came out of the Aleutians in December to redeem the point's oily annus horribilis of 1969. It was a wave like no other and only a few brave souls (Yater, Kevin Sears, George Greenough, Jeff Boyd, and Stu Fredericks among them) dared to face a swell breaking so far offshore that merely paddling out risked drowning.

And finally, not every guy or gal who carries a board may surf Rincon. Locals know they must hone their skills elsewhere before joining the lineup. In the 1970s and 1980s, the point was defended against a multicolored-wetsuit army of interlopers from Los Angeles. Although those days of hyper-localism and beach fistfights are gone, holy ground is still worth protecting from desecration, whatever its form!

Among those posing in this c. 1938 photograph on Carpinteria Beach are pith-helmeted lifeguards Gates Foss (1915–1990) and Myron "Mike" Sturmer (died 2011), second and third from the right. Both Sturmer and Foss surfed Rincon prewar, with the latter likely the first Anglo American to do so. These early boards were either hollow paddleboards or slightly shorter solid redwood planks. (Courtesy Martha Dowling Rodriguez.)

A lone surfer exits Rincon Cove around 1952 as a freight train rumbles past. This photograph is an almost wistful picture of the quiet before the "gremmie" invasion that brought *Gidget*-crazed neophyte surfers to the point beginning in the late 1950s. Despite this onslaught and almost 75 years of near constant change at the point since this photograph was taken, the view is identical today. (Courtesy Dick Metz/ SHACC Archives.)

A requirement of surfing in the pre-wetsuit era was a fire on the beach, like the one Santa Barbara surf legend Billy Meng (born 1930) tends here, where surfers could warm themselves after emerging from the cold Rincon waters. Meng and his crew would find old tires along the highway, start them alight on the beach, and then use the warmed sand for sleeping until day broke and they could surf again. (Courtesy Dick Metz/ SHACC Archives.)

After weeks of work off Rincon Cove in the fall of 1958, proud skindivers (from left to right) John Besand, Kenneth Williams, Jerry Clausen, and Bob Clausen) pose with the anchor they pulled from 15 feet of water about 150 yards offshore. Among the most famous discoveries in the Santa Barbara Channel is the 1981 find at Goleta Beach of five 600-pound cannons believed to date to the 18th century. Their origins—like this anchor—remain uncertain. (Courtesy Halsted family.)

A well-worn scrapbook of photographs and enthusiastic musings about the Rincon scene captured a pivotal moment in surfing's rise in California, just as it began the transition from an outlaw sport for rebels like Dick Metz to a mainstream activity backed by a just-forming wave of films, television, and music. Created by frequent point visitor Jason Lumley, the scrapbook was given to the Halsted family in 1957 in thanks for hosting him. Filling its pages are photos of Lumley's buddies taking to the Rincon waves more than 60 years ago. One of the surfers featured is Ken Kesson (1928–2015), captured here around 1957, one of Santa Barbara and Ventura's founding fathers of surf. Among his many accomplishments, Kesson helped found the Santa Barbara County Surf Club in 1960 to open up Hollister Ranch as a treasured surf spot. About the time of this photograph, Kesson appeared in a local newspaper extolling his sport for the uninitiated: "Surfing is addicting like no other sport I know . . . The joy and thrill, the perfect mental therapy of the cold water and the racing board, this exhilarating effect makes surfing one of the most purely relaxing sports I know." Kesson went on to compete in still-iconic surf contests, including the US Surfing Championship in 1964 at Huntington Beach and in Peru the following year at the World Surfing Championship. Note his "Rincon" t-shirt. (Courtesy Halsted family.)

This snapshot was labeled "One of the better winter surfs in '59." Thanks to the print and film versions of *Gidget* and their progeny, there were now more than a few surfers in the Rincon waters. (Courtesy Halsted family.)

Eric Arneson is pictured at Rincon Point in 1965. The shot was taken by Carpinteria photographer and surfer Bill Robbins (born 1945). Robbins learned surf photography from mentor LeRoy Grannis. The grace and joy of Arneson's pose is reminiscent of the famous *Surfer* magazine logo and image from 1959 showing Kemp Aaberg in a perfect soul arch, also at Rincon. (Courtesy Bill Robbins.)

These photographs were taken by LeRoy Grannis at Rincon Point. The *New York Times* called Grannis (1917–2011) the "godfather of surf photography." He took early to surfing and probably began taking surf photographs in the 1940s, but it was his work in the 1960s that helped shape the sport and culture's golden age. Grannis left behind many photographs of Rincon Point, most of which are in the SHACC archive. Pictured above is a typical Rincon day in the early 1960s. Below, Grannis captures Wayne Miyata (1942–2005) at Rincon around 1962. Miyata was an influential native Hawaiian surfer who appeared in *Endless Summer* and designed, built, and decorated surfboards with artwork influenced by his love of samurai culture. (Both, courtesy Grannis family and SHACC.)

This iconic image, taken by Ron Stoner in December 1966, shows, from left to right, John Peck (born 1944), Miki Dora (1934–2002), and Denny Aaberg (born 1947). All three are surfing legends, with the scheming, work-shy, and charismatic Dora still the most famous surfer of all time. Although Dora's home base was Malibu, he was often spotted at Rincon Point. At the time of this photograph, Dora stood at the height of his powers, the reigning "King of Malibu," appearing in surfing contests (often not faring as well as he thought he should), in surf flicks and magazines, and frequently on the party circuit. His adoring fans treated his occasional sermon-on-the-mount-style declarations as holy writ, to be deconstructed and worried over like Beatles lyrics. In a 1967 *Surfer* article, for example, Dora claimed that Malibu had been ruined by an influx of kooks. The boards pictured here are almost as famous as their riders. According to designer and historian Paul Gross, "Peck is riding a Morey Pope Penetrator, with its signature twin stringers, turned down front rails, and Slipcheck [a traction compound] nose. Denny has a super clean Lance Carson Model. Dora's board was either the original Yater Spoon, or one of the first few. It was reportedly 9 feet 2 inches which was very short at the time . . . The deck had been pigmented white to cover all the ding repairs from heavy use. This board is thought to be the inspiration for Greg Noll's 'Da Cat' model." (Photograph by Ron Stoner; courtesy SHACC.)

The endpapers of the Carpinteria High School yearbook in 1967 captured a golden moment in Rincon surf history with this photograph of a good portion of Rincon's greatest local surfing generation. The boys are, from left to right, Bernie Baker, Kent Williams, Bill Wheeler, Jeff Boyd, and Mark Campbell. The girls are, from left to right, Barbara Swing, Sarah Christie, Shelley Milne, Linda Gonzales, Jeanne Russell, and Pam Cleveland. Other exceptional surfers of this generation include Kevin Sears (class of 1967), Chris Blakeslee, Steve Johnson (1970), Matt Moore (1970), and Scott Gall (1971). Note that Wheeler, Boyd, and Campbell all wear Hope Ranch

Surf Club surf trunks. Baker, who became a photographer and masthead editor at *Surfer*, said of this photograph's zeitgeist, "I have lived that moment in time all my life." He was referring not so much to this sunny day with friends at the beach, but to his entire early life in Carpinteria, a youth spent in the waves or riding his bike (and lugging a massive longboard) along the railroad tracks to get in a quick surf at the point after school. For Baker and other high school seniors in this photograph, surfing was not just a youthful pastime but a lifelong commitment. (Courtesy Jim Campos.)

Mark Campbell (born 1949) is seen at Rincon around 1966. Like others in this storied surfing class, Campbell went to Hawaii after graduation to combine a love of surfing with higher education. He later became a treasure hunter and elementary schoolteacher. Here he is on his nine-foot, two-inch Yater Spoon. Says Campbell, "You could plant yourself on the nose of those boards and stay there all day long on those runners in the Cove." (Courtesy Jim Campos.)

Jeff Boyd, pictured around 1967 at Rincon Cove, is making a radical bottom turn with his fin out of the water. Riding the longboard like a shortboard, Boyd pointed the way to the coming shortboard revolution. Boyd said, "The board was a Yater that was about 9'6" . . . My friend Kevin Sears on occasion borrowed that board and I always thought it might have been him in the photo . . . It's a great photo and it's either Kevin or me." (Courtesy Steve Bissell.)

Above, George Greenough (born 1941) rides his revolutionary self-designed kneeboard at Rincon Point in 1969. Sometimes called the "barefoot mad genius" of surfing, Greenough was one of the point's great characters. But do not let eccentricities mask his physical and creative talents. Besides being a star surfer in his own right, Greenough developed designs to surf the way he wanted. Then, he revolutionized surf cinematography by inventing the tools and techniques to record the action the way he wanted. In a still stunning film sequence, Greenough anticipated the GoPro era by almost 50 years when he became the first to capture the view from "inside the barrel" on video by lugging a 28-pound camera and housing into the waves. The sequence starred in his film *The Innermost Limits of Pure Fun* (1970). At right is Greenough in Hawaii during the filming of *Big Wednesday* in 1977. (Above, courtesy Harold Wardie Ward; right, courtesy Don Balch.)

Here is Steve Bissell's iconic and widely published photograph of Rincon Point. It originally appeared as a two-page pull-out centerfold in *Surfer*; the mini-poster hung in hundreds of surfers' rooms in the 1970s. The story goes that after a particularly beautiful day at the point in 1973, photographer Bissell (born 1947) had the idea to see what the view might be from the top of Rincon Hill. This masterpiece was the result, with Bissell's friend Gary Ward nicely framing the shot. Since Bissell had trespassed to get the photograph, he was worried when Robert Bates called and asked him to appear at his ranch. Fortunately, Bates merely wanted a copy of the photo. The combination of Bissell's Rincon Hill photograph and Don Balch's 1981 christening of Rincon as "the Queen of the Coast" did much to solidify the point's status as one of the world's greatest surf spots. (Courtesy Steve Bissell.)

IS THIS? STAN THi MAN COWAN?

Stan Cowan (born 1957) is seen at the point about 1980 on his Al Merrick–designed Channel Islands board. As a young teenager, Stan's routine for a weekday Rincon surf was a bike ride from his home to the bluffs to inspect the waves, a quick return home to request his mom call him in sick at school, and then a hitchhike with board to Bates Road. (Courtesy Cowan family.)

This early version of the Rincon Pit Crew on the point's east side, pictured around 1980, includes, from left to right, Rob Witton, Dennis Russell-Hurd (born 1949), Mike Lane, and professional football player Jack Turnbull (1950–2020). According to Russell-Hurd, the key to the Pit Crew's longevity has been "maintaining a good vibe." (Courtesy Dennis Russell-Hurd.)

SURFER

JUNE
VOL. 22, NO. 6
$2.50

The Queen of the Coast
RINCON'S GLORIOUS REIGN

Riders on the Storm
JOURNEYS THROUGH INDONESIA'S HEART OF DARKNESS

Island Music
A SYMPHONY FROM THE SEA

In a stroke of genius with far-reaching impact, Don Balch (born 1952) titled his June 1981 *Surfer* article, "La Rinconada del Mar: The Queen of the Coast," setting in motion an honorific title for the point that would stick. Besides the catchy headline in this issue of the magazine, Balch's article is noteworthy for its snapshot of the 1981 cultural moment at Rincon, complete with electronic-gate-card moochers, "locals only" tribalism, and a heartfelt homage to the place's regulars. (Courtesy Don Balch.)

Rincon regular Simone Reddingius (born 1957) sets up at Backside Rincon in the early 1980s. Besides photography, Reddingius is also a surfer, musician, and painter. Her work has appeared in *Surfing* and *Surfer* magazines. Always torn about whether to surf or photograph first, Reddingius says surfing usually wins out. (Courtesy Simone Reddingius.)

In a photograph taken from the water, Tom Curren (born 1964) is in action at Rincon Point around 1983. Curren is a three-time world champion whose father, Pat Curren (born 1932), was also surf royalty. (Courtesy Jimmy Metyko.)

They are not jumping for joy at the long run of good surf at Rincon during the early 1980s, but might as well be. Between 1980 and 1983, photographer Jimmy Metyko (born 1959) captured both the surf and the cultural moment at Rincon and the surrounding area. Here, he catches young local surfers on Rincon Hill. From left to right are Dana McCorkle, Matt Mondragon, Gabriel Novoa, Tim Smalley, and Josh Klein. (Courtesy Jimmy Metyko.)

Al Merrick (born 1944) discusses Channel Islands boards, technique, and waves with three young acolytes at Rincon Point around 1983. Jimmy Metyko's photographs from the early 1980s captured the unique partnership forged between designer and master shaper Merrick and surf phenom Tom Curren. (Courtesy Jimmy Metyko.)

Titled "Waiting for Low Tide," this iconic c. 1983 photograph shows colorful wetsuits drying on a Buick Skylark at the Rincon Point parking lot. (Courtesy Jimmy Metyko.)

Frequent Rincon Classic standout Lisa Luna is seen at Rincon Point in 1985. Notwithstanding a few notable exceptions, relatively few women were in the Rincon waves before the 1980s, when the gender balance finally began to shift. (Courtesy Simone Reddingius)

Here is Rincon veteran Tim Smalley as captured by Simone Reddingius from the water at the point in 1986. (Courtesy Simone Reddingius.)

Rincon regulars enjoy the first and only Queen of the Coast Longboard Classic of January 1987 from the comfort of their palapa. At center in leggings is Mara Tucker, a standout surfer and later an advocate for cleaning up Rincon's water. (Courtesy Don Balch.)

Finalists of the Queen of the Coast Longboard Classic of 1987 are, from left to right, Mike Emerson, Jonathan Paskowitz, Jay Riddle (first place), Herbie Fletcher, Chris Olivas, and Dale Dobson. The black-and-white reproduction does not do these multicolored wetsuits justice. (Courtesy Don Balch.)

Surf legend Kim Mearig (born 1963) is photographed from the water by friend Simone Reddingius at Rincon Point in 1986. Like former classmate Tom Curren, Mearig was long associated with Al Merrick's Channel Islands. She won the 1981 US Surfing Championships. (Courtesy Simone Reddingius.)

The 2002 Rincon Classic featured memorably big surf, which was said to grow from two feet to ten feet during the day. It got so big that the groms' categories were put in danger for safety reasons until some parents swam out to serve as lifeguards for the younger competitors. Here, Oliver Parker takes advantage of the big waves. (Courtesy John Nordstrand.)

Simone Reddingius is on the nose of a longboard at Rincon Point in 2016. A frequent standout at the Rincon Classic, Reddingius placed second in the 2022 Lady Legends category. After a chance meeting with Denny Aaberg at Carpinteria State Beach in 1973, Simone became hooked on surfing for life. When not surfing or photographing surfing, Reddingius performs with Aaberg in the surf band The Wrinkled Teenagers. (Photograph by Duncan Mckenzie, courtesy Simone Reddingius.)

Titled "70 is the new 20," Carpinteria photographer David Powdrell catches ageless Rincon legend Andy Neumann (born 1946) at the 2017 iteration of the Rincon Classic. (Courtesy David Powdrell.)

Nine

RESIDENTS AND HOMES

Here is a look at some of Rincon Point's more noteworthy residents—early arrivals as well as celebrities—and their avocations and celebrations, plus a few vanished homes of Rinconers long gone.

For nearly a century, the point has been a magnet for the arts and their creators. *Architectural Digest* editor Paige Rense lived here, as did two writers who appear below, Silvia Dobson and Barnaby Conrad. Artists who have lived at Rincon Point include Richard S. Meryman, who appears in chapter six, as well as Barnaby Conrad (a writer-artist) and Jack Baker, who are seen in this chapter.

Many Rincon Point notables have been involved with entertainment. In addition to Warner Oland, who appears below, Kevin Costner had a house on the beach, though longtime resident Mary Conrad remembers him as "just a movie star who came for the weekends." Others include Susan Harris, creator of *Golden Girls* and other shows; Tony Thomas, producer of *Dead Poets Society* (and son of Danny Thomas and brother of Marlo Thomas); and cinematographer and director Louie Schwartzberg.

Still others have passed through. D.W. Griffith and Lillian Gish dined at the Rincon Inn in 1919, a year before Prohibition made it infamous. Guests at the Conrad house on Rincon Creek, in Mary's recollection, include actors Robert Mitchum, Jane Russell, Stewart Granger, Roddy MacDowell, José Ferrer, and Vivian Vance. Jack Baker's parties featured Loretta Young, Bradford Dillman, Dame Judith Anderson, and Eva Marie Saint.

Not that one had to be a celebrity to draw attention. At Rincon Point's annual Fourth of July celebration, children dressed as Indians listened as their elders listed the rules of their ersatz tribe—most notably, "Rincon Indians don't throw sand."

We close the chapter with a look at several memorable houses, including two from the early 1900s—a late Craftsman bungalow and a squatter's beach shack.

Like some Rincon Point residents today, Joaquin Murietta had many homes. One hideout in the 1850s was said to be a cave located above the beach just west of the point; it was later destroyed by railroad construction. A map supposedly showed a chest of diamonds that Murietta buried, by an oak tree marked with a cross near three white rocks. Some treasure-hunters figured it must be around Rincon Creek, and residents and workers periodically found deep holes beside trees. (Courtesy California State Library.)

Warner Oland, a Swedish-born actor who achieved incongruous movie fame playing Chinese master detective Charlie Chan, moved to Rincon Point with his wife, Edith, in the 1920s. They attended parties, entertained Boy Scouts, took young Bobette Bates to a movie premiere in a limousine, and distributed autographed photographs. This one went to Robert W. Bates. (Courtesy Bates family.)

Warner Oland trains or taunts one of his dogs at Rincon Point. In 1937, three Oland dogs attacked the Bates family's dog, Monty. In trying to separate them, Oland and Robert Bates ended up tangled on the ground, "both puffing like steam engines, with me on top," Bates recounted, adding, "I am glad it was not the other way around." A movie magazine, he thought, would have paid handsomely for a photograph. (Courtesy Warner Oland Archives, Bjurholm, Sweden.)

Ultimately, the Olands owned several houses on Rincon Point. This cottage, now owned by the Lindley Foundation, is the only one still standing. Warner and Edith Oland split up in 1937, and a sheriff's officer served legal papers on Warner while he was sunbathing. He died in 1938, and Edith sold the last of her Rincon properties in 1951. (Courtesy Bates family.)

In 1934, Silvia Dobson, shown here, became a lover of the modernist poet H.D. (Hilda Doolittle). After the sexual relationship ended, according to Dobson, "an enchanted friendship" endured. In 1964, Dobson and her partner, Liz Truelson, moved to Rincon Point. They had long talks with Robert W. Bates and a Mr. Hill, probably Edwin, about the point's history. The two men did not care for each other, according to Dobson, but "we loved them both." (Courtesy Diana Collecott.)

After Liz Truelson died in 1980, Silvia Dobson paid hefty taxes on "the house we built together, shared, and left to one another in our wills," because the law then treated gay couples as strangers. Here, Dobson (left) sits with Betty Shoemaker, who moved in after Truelson's death. Dobson suspected that other Rincon Point women were lesbians, but they were "so tightly closeted that we never tried to penetrate their isolation." (Courtesy Schlesinger Library, Harvard Radcliffe Institute.)

Rincon Point resident Barnaby Conrad compressed many lives into his 90 years—bullfighter in Spain, known as El Niño de California; personal secretary to Nobel-winner Sinclair Lewis; author of the novel *Matador*, published in 1952, which sold three million copies; portrait and landscape painter; owner of a nightclub in San Francisco; teacher at the Cate School; and founder, with his wife, Mary, of the Santa Barbara Writer's Conference. In this photograph from 2011, he sits by his painting "El Matador." An essay by Conrad, published in 2004, describes the view from his Rincon Point patio: The sun is bright, a dozen surfers ride waves, dolphins splash in the distance, and a paraglider floats overhead. When Mary suggests a trip to Europe, Barnaby replies, "Why travel? We are here!" (Courtesy Fran Collin.)

Barnaby and Mary Conrad received the house lot by Rincon Creek as a wedding gift from his mother in 1963. They built a house there for vacations while they lived in San Francisco, and then they expanded it and moved there permanently in 1973. One of Barnaby's seascapes hangs over the mantel in the book-filled living room. (Courtesy Mary Conrad.)

Visitors to Barnaby and Mary Conrad's house included novelist James Michener, shown here with their daughter Kendall, as well as writers Alex Haley, Eudora Welty, William Styron, Ray Bradbury, Joan Didion, Kenneth Rexroth, Jackie Collins, Fannie Flagg, and Clive Cussler, according to Kendall and Mary Conrad. Barnaby's portraits of Michener, Haley, and Truman Capote are in the collection of the National Portrait Gallery in Washington. (Courtesy Mary Conrad.)

The artist Jack Baker bought a former carriage house on Rincon Point Road and lived there until his death in 2011. On evening walks, he sometimes spotted shoots of asparagus rising from the soil, which he believed were sprouting from seeds left behind by the Hill family 100 years earlier. (Courtesy Fran Collin.)

Jack Baker established his reputation in the 1960s with bright paintings of flowers. At Rincon Point, he often painted what he saw around him, including this young surfer. (Courtesy India Baker.)

Thacher family and friends enjoy a picnic in 1941. Beginning third from left are Harriet Thacher Herrick with son Newby Herrick and daughter Heidi Herrick, Phil Thacher, Helen Thacher (in hat), and Elizabeth Thacher. In the background is the Edward Bates home. Elizabeth's father, Sherman Day Thacher (1861–1931), founded the Thacher School in 1889. (Courtesy Thacher family.)

Angler Margaret Pascoe Thacher (1909–1995) shows off an impressive catch at Rincon Point around 1960. The fish are likely opaleye perch. In 1933, she married Anson Thacher, longtime headmaster of Thacher School. (Courtesy Thacher family.)

At right, Christopher Halsted plays "To the Colors" while a dog guards the coast and Steve Halsted raises Old Glory to mark the beginning of the 1971 Fourth of July celebrations at Rincon Point. Below are initiates to the Rincon Indians at the annual Fourth of July celebration around 1967. The faux ceremonies sought to connect modern Rincon with the prehistoric world at a time when archaeological excavations at the point were relatively frequent. Initiation rites included instruction and admonishments to new members, including the requirement that "Rincon Indians don't throw sand" and mastery of the traditional greeting and response: "How's the weather? / Clammy! / Where? / Rincon Point!" (Both, courtesy Halsted family.)

In the 1910s, Tony Peraz lived in a wooden shack on the beach, probably the one seen above through the fog. When Robert W. Bates tried to evict him, he contended that he occupied unclaimed land. The boundaries of the Bates property, and those of the Rancho El Rincon land grant as a whole, were ambiguous. Under Bates's interpretation, the property ran to the seashore, whereas under Peraz's interpretation, the property ended several feet above high tide. Bates filed suit. Peraz, evidently a squatter of means, retained a surveyor, who drew the map below, and a lawyer. After visiting the shack, studying maps, and hearing testimony, a Ventura County judge ruled for Bates. According to newspaper accounts, the ruling gave landowners along the central coast the authority to expel hundreds of squatters. (Above, courtesy Robbie Hutto; below, courtesy Ventura County Court.)

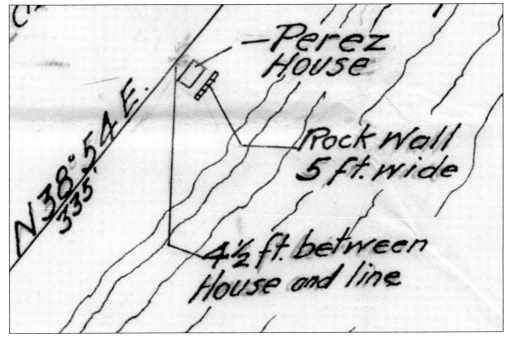

Here is the former 6721 South Via Real, "the little red shack," showing the fireplace and chimney of beach/river stone and local pottery sherds. The home was rented by Don and Helen White from Esolina Hill West (1892–1984) between 1959 and 1965. (Courtesy Doug White.)

The former 6723 South Via Real belonged to Esolina Hill West. A 1980 survey speculated the English cottage–style home might have been transported from a different site. West always warned residents and visitors to beware the south swell, because her first husband had drowned at Rincon in 1912, shortly after their marriage. In 1917, she married William Henry West and lived near Clovis, California, before returning to Rincon after his death. (Courtesy Doug White.)

The Hill family home at 6701 South Via Real was the most prominent of all the homes at Rincon Point for decades. The Bateses lived in the small house briefly, and Katharine Mitchell Bates (Robert and Edward's mother) died there in 1919. Carmelita Hill Rhodes (1887–1982), shown at left, lived in the home for many years. A typical late Craftsman bungalow, the home replaced the Hills' prior residence on the point, which was lost in a storm. The long flight of concrete stairs to the cottage is all that remains of the house, which was demolished in the early 1980s. (Above, courtesy Doug White; left, courtesy Carpinteria Valley Museum of History.)

Carmelita Hill is shown as a young woman around 1907 with Hill family friend Bill Bennett at Rincon Point. (Courtesy Suzanne Rhodes.)

Pictured in 1969, Suzanne Rhodes (left) is with grandmother Carmelita Hill Rhodes at Rincon Point. (Courtesy Suzanne Rhodes.)

Three generations of Halsteds (from left to right, Steve, Christopher, and A. Stevens) pose with a wayward oil company buoy in 1966. In the background is the Edwin Ardell Hill house (built around 1920) at 6713 South Via Real. Hill (1903–1981) had pig pens, chicken coops, and vegetable gardens on the west side of the point for many years. The wooden platform in the background was used as a defensive gun emplacement during World War II. (Courtesy Halsted family.)

Below the Ardell Hill house is a home associated with Perry Irwin. Irwin's father loved to fish and would drive an old gray jeep along the beach to his fishing spot, posing a threat to anything in his path since he did not see well. In the foreground are remains of a totemic carving by Vern Rice, another Hill estate character who lived in a garage owned by Esolina West and who fired a small cannon out to sea on holidays. (Courtesy Spector family.)

Ten

CHALLENGES IN PARADISE

For a place sometimes called paradise and likened to a queen, it may be blasphemy to suggest the 30-odd acres of Rincon Point have ever had significant problems. But like anywhere people congregate, challenges of the man-made variety abound. Among the threats to the point's beauty and calm covered in these pages are flooding, proximity to hydrocarbons and their extraction, wildfire, the preservation of native flora and fauna, and how to accommodate so many beachgoers with differing priorities, including local and non-local surfers, nude sunbathers, paragliders, saltwater anglers, and miscellaneous other Rincon-lovers. Two other challenges go hand-in-hand and are also due to Rincon's popularity—over-development and sewage pollution. The first of these challenges is largely settled now that all buildable lots have been developed; however, the issue of short-term rentals remains a challenge. In terms of sanitation, or what has been called the "effluent of the affluent" problem, a 15-year battle to replace the point's leaky septic tanks with a connection to a modern sewage system finally ended in 2014 with residents ponying up $5.2 million for a state-of-the-art system. There is even occasional crime at the point, and this chapter ends with a terrible deed that put Rincon on the map as a murder scene. All these threats have put the queen at risk of being loved to death. So far, however, the place seems to be holding up and remains one of the most beloved and beautiful beaches in California.

Rincon Point was created by its namesake creek, and what the creek gives, it can take away. For example, on January 25, 1914, the Santa Barbara newspaper recorded that "the Dr. R.W. Hill place, landmark of the Rincon road, has been washed into the sea. The house, barn, outbuildings, and the magnificent sycamore, are gone." The Hills claimed the flooding was due to the railroad's rerouting of the creek, and they prevailed on Southern Pacific to replace their home, which was wisely placed on higher ground. A dozen years later, an April 1926 flood knocked the Bates family structures off their moorings. Robert Bates captured the aftermath in a homemade film showing necktie-wearing Bates men cleaning up. This is a still from the film. Storms, sometimes accompanied by punishing surf, continue to threaten property at the point, with notable recent rains in 2005, 1998, 1995, 1983, 1978, and 1969. (Courtesy Bates family.)

Above is the scene on Rincon beach after a February 1958 storm. Both February and March 1958 were rainy months in a wet year. Pictured below is the "Pole House" of Elizabeth Truelson and Silvia Dobson at Rincon Creek during the epic floods of January 1969. The wooden shed at right is at the approximate site of the current yard of 1 Rincon Point Lane. According to longtime Rincon residents, the shed was occupied in the 1960s–1970s by a solitary man who usually cooked outside (the shack had no kitchen) to the delight of local dogs. (Above, courtesy Halsted family; below, courtesy Doug White.)

Just visible is steam or smoke from the "Rincon Volcano," a fissure on Rincon Hill that has emitted hot and odorous gasses, smoke, and steam in numerous "eruptions," including in 1835, 1866, 1877, 1944, and 1982. An attraction of sorts, tourists were sometimes treated to staged eruptions, and boosters in Ventura and Santa Barbara chided each other over ownership of and responsibility for the "hot hole." Famed local geologist Thomas Dibblee (1911–2004) explained the phenomenon as a deep crevice of flammable oil shale. (Courtesy Peter Hunt.)

Here is the just-completed artificial Rincon oil island in April 1959. Considered an engineering feat at the time of its construction—its massive concrete "tetrapods" dissipate the force of incoming waves—the island, which is sometimes called the ninth Channel Island, gradually became a burden for its corporate owners. By 2021, all the oil wells on the island had been decommissioned, and the state had taken possession. The final fate of the artificial island remains in doubt. (Courtesy Halsted family.)

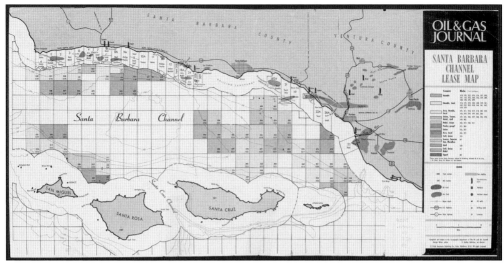

A 1968 Santa Barbara Channel map of then-current oil fields and leases documents the area's 1960s oil boom. As many as 75 offshore platforms were planned. But after the spill of 1969, future projects met massive resistance. Those platforms closest to Rincon Point today are four adjacent to Summerland (named, from east to west, Hillhouse, A, B, and C), three adjacent to Carpinteria (Hogan, Houchin, and Henry), and an eighth (Habitat) farther offshore. (Courtesy Special Research Collections, UC Santa Barbara Library.)

A blowout at Union Oil Company's Platform A on January 28, 1969, brought the local oil boom to a screeching halt. The spill killed countless seabirds and mammals and fouled beaches from Goleta to Ventura, including Rincon Point. Outcry over the disaster helped launch the environmental movement nationally, as well as local anti-oil activism. Here, Union Oil crews remove oil-soaked debris from the east side of Rincon Point. (Courtesy Halsted family.)

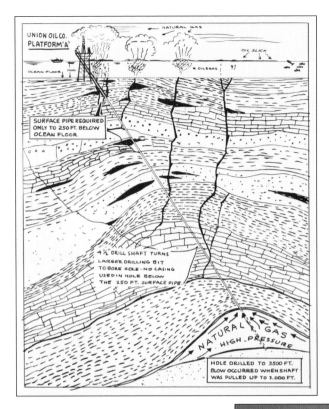

This diagram from the aftermath of the spill gives the particulars of the disaster, including rock layers in the area below the platform. The lucrative pockets of oil and gas are shown, as well as the approximate location of the blowout. (Courtesy Get Oil Out [GOO] Collection, Special Research Collections, UC Santa Barbara Library.)

Since at least the 1970s, an area between the Venoco pier and the county park has been an on-again, off-again clothing-optional beach. Aside from a period between about 2000 and 2008, when sheriffs handed out tickets to nudists, an unofficial "look the other way" policy has prevailed, despite this current sign. The clothing-optional case is advocated by Friends of Bates Beach. (Courtesy Burns family.)

A massive pyrocumulus, or "fire cloud," towers over the Carpinteria valley during the July 1985 Wheeler Fire. The fire broke out in the Los Padres backcountry on July 1 and burned 118,000 acres and 40 percent of the Rincon Creek drainage before containment. Other wildfires that approached Rincon Point were the Romero (1971) and Thomas (2017–2018) fires. The latter caused evacuations and produced weeks of yellow, smokey air at Rincon Point. It jumped the 101 freeway to burn palm trees on its ocean side south of Rincon Point. (Courtesy Burns family.)

Rincon Point sometimes struggles to coexist with its wildlife. Pictured above on August 19, 2017, a mature black bear appeared on Rincon beach to the surprise of beachgoers. It had likely wandered down Rincon Creek under the freeway and through the tunnel from higher country in the Los Padres National Forest, a remarkable journey. California Fish and Wildlife staff tranquilized the bear, determined it to be in poor health, and euthanized it. Other rare and not-so-rare visitors to the point include turtles, foxes, osprey, bald eagles, egrets, herons, and a wide variety of other shore and ocean birds. Pinnipeds like the sea lion pictured below in 1983 will occasionally seek refuge from storms at oceanfront homes. Very rarely, as in prehistoric times, a dead whale may wash up on the beach, a joyous event for the Chumash because it meant abundant meat. (Above, courtesy Larry Clark; below, courtesy Burns family.)

A newspaper notice from June 7, 1875, offered a reward for the arrest, delivery, and conviction of John "Jack" Cotton and Caroline Norton for the murder of Norton's husband, John, in April 1875 at Rincon Point, a salacious crime involving a love triangle with a young mother (Caroline Norton), a scheming hired man (Cotton), and a victim who was known to beat his wife (John Norton). When searchers found John Norton's battered body in a Rincon sand dune, the guilty pair went on the run. This photograph of the murderers played a pivotal role in their Santa Barbara trial since it suggested the pair were intimate. The silk dress bought by Norton for the photograph cost $140. The case and the ensuing trial occupied Santa Barbara throughout the spring and summer, with fallout continuing for years. (Right, courtesy California Digital Newspaper Collection; below, courtesy Gledhill Library, Santa Barbara Historical Museum.)

$500 Reward!

STATE OF CALIFORNIA, EXECU-tive Department, Sacramento, June 1st 1875. Whereas on or about the fifteenth day of April, A. D. 1875, John Norton was murdered by one John Cotton, aided and abetted by one Mrs. Caroline Norton, now the reputed wife of the said John Cotton, the crime having been committed in the County of Santa Barbara in this State and the said murderers are still at large and undiscovered.

Now, therefore by virtue of authority in me vested, I, Romualdo Pacheco, Governor of California, do hereby offer a Reward of Five Hundred Dollars for the arrest of the said John Cotton and Caroline Norton, payable upon their delivery to the Sheriff of Santa Barbara County and conviction of said crime of murder.

In testimony whereof I have hereunto set my hand and caused the Great Seal of the state to be affixed at Sacramento, California, this 1st day of June, A. D. 1875.

[SEAL.]

ROMUALDO PACHECO,
Governor.

Attest:

DRURY MELONE,
Secretary of the State.

DESCRIPTION.

JOHN COTTON, Aged about 35 years at out 5 feet 7 inches in height; dark complexion, black mustache and chin whiskers; rather thick set with down cast countenance and heavy eyebrows.

CAROLINE NORTON, Aged about 26 years; is about 5 feet 5 inches in height; a demi-blonde; light auburn hair, with a bunch of grey near the poll of the head on the under side, the color caused from an injury; short upper lip; teeth slightly irregular; she had two children with her when last heard from, a girl and a boy.

The Girl is named Susan about 6 or 7 years old; light hair slightly curly, blue eye, rather pensive in gaze. The boy is about 3 or 4 years of age; dark complexion; thick set; is named John Edward.

DISCOVER THOUSANDS OF LOCAL HISTORY BOOKS FEATURING MILLIONS OF VINTAGE IMAGES

Arcadia Publishing, the leading local history publisher in the United States, is committed to making history accessible and meaningful through publishing books that celebrate and preserve the heritage of America's people and places.

Find more books like this at
www.arcadiapublishing.com

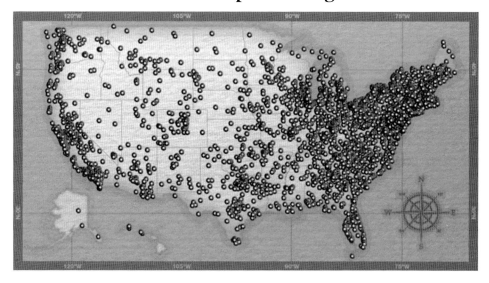

Search for your hometown history, your old stomping grounds, and even your favorite sports team.

Consistent with our mission to preserve history on a local level, this book was printed in South Carolina on American-made paper and manufactured entirely in the United States. Products carrying the accredited Forest Stewardship Council (FSC) label are printed on 100 percent FSC-certified paper.

MADE IN THE
USA